STORES
OF THE YEAR

no.20

RSD Publishing. Inc., 102 Cove Road, South Salem, NY

Disclaimer: The majority of images in this publication were provided to RSD Publishing by the Retail Design Institute and, in some instances, additional images were obtained from the project designer. In almost all cases the Retail Design Institute also provided design and supplier credit information supplied to them on submittal forms entered in the 43rd International Store Design Competition. RSD Publishing has made every effort via email and the Internet to verify addresses and other information in the designers, architect and advertiser index. RSD can accept no responsibility for factual or typographical errors in data provided by RDI or others on submittal forms for this publication.

RSD Publishing, Inc.
102 Cove Road
S.Salem, NY 10590
917-596-7595
jburr@rsdpublishing.com
www.rdimedia.com

Distributors to the trade in the United States and Canada
Innovative Logistics, LLC.
406 Wycoff Mills Road
East Windsor, NJ 08520
In USA: 866-289-2088
Outside USA: 732-363-4511

Library of Congress Cataloging in Publication Data:
Stores of the Year No. 20

Book & Jacket Design: Martina Marie Parisi
Editor: John Hogan

Printed and Bound in Hong Kong
ISBN: 978-0-9854674-4-9

40 YEARS OF
BOLD

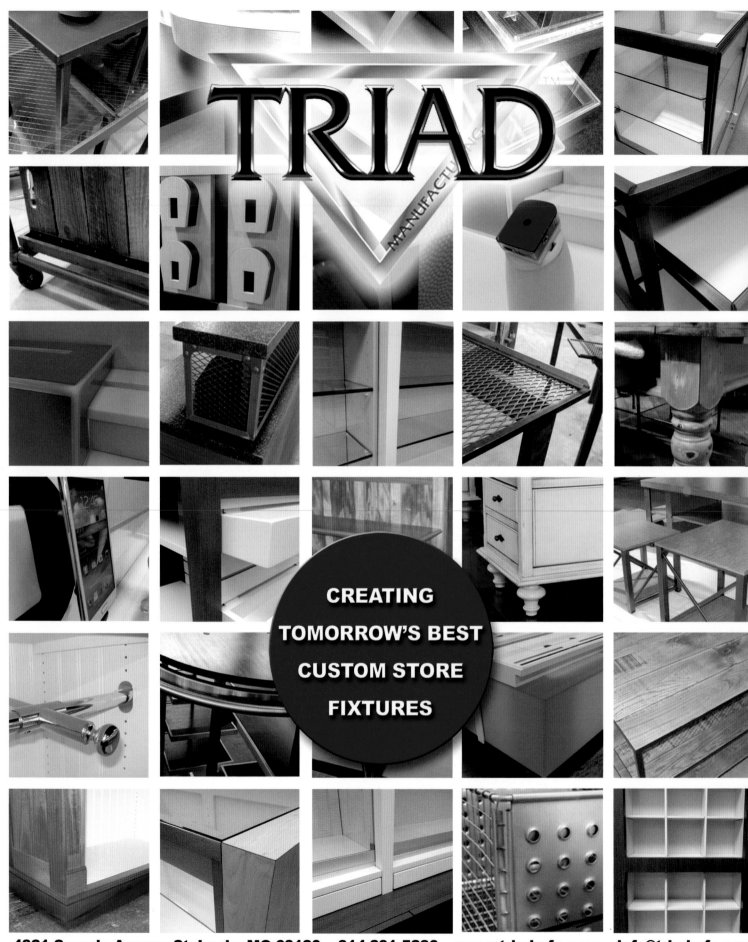

CREATING
TOMORROW'S BEST
CUSTOM STORE
FIXTURES

TABLE OF CONTENTS

Retail Design International Store Design Competition

Happy Birthday Mondo Mannequins

In 1989, Econoco Corporation started Mondo Mannequins; a company dedicated to producing the finest quality mannequins and forms. Mondo's experience results from decades of supplying display forms to the retail industry under it's original corporate name.

25 years later, Mondo Mannequins supplies the most well known apparel brands, and department and specialty store chains with the world's most fashionable and trendsetting visual displays.

In the display department of Gimbels Department Store, New York City, Display Director John E. Saporita (right) directs staff artist-designer John Teeple in dressing one of the new Athena torso forms. At left is Arthur Zelniker, president of the Economy Cover Corporation, Jamaica, L. I., N. Y., developers of the amazing new forms made of a special plastic composition that cannot be dented, scuffed or scraped, yet readily accepts pins. The forms were created after 3½ years of research and experimentation.

Reprinted from DISPLAY WORLD magazine, April 1965.

Mondo is pleased to announce its partnership with Genesis Mannequins of Germany. Together we have created a global brand offering world-wide distribution and cutting edge designs made with eco-friendly bio-resin materials.

We look forward to celebrating our 25th Birthday with you.

MONDO
MANNEQUINS

mondomannequins.com   www.genesis-display.com

FOREWORD

"The Retail Design Institute promotes the advancement and collaborative practice of creating selling environments."

This is not just the Institute's vision statement, but also our call to action. Now in its 53rd year, the Institute continues to set the standards of the profession and is the arbiter of great design solutions. Our broad based membership represents all the collaborative disciplines needed to create innovative retail experiences that build on customer loyalty, deliver on the brand promise and provide the planning and design solutions that increase sales.

Stores of the Year 20 is a celebration of our passion, retail design, and this year's winners are the "best of the best" for 2013. These projects required the seamless integration of retail disciplines and are judged against a set of criteria which all have to measure highly in the judges' scoring: concept, store planning, lighting, merchandise presentation/fixturing, graphics, and materials. But most importantly, they speak to the expertise of the people who work together under tight schedules to deliver successful, beautiful spaces on time and on budget; the retailers, the contractors and design consultants.

Congratulations to this year's winners and to the teams behind the work.

Andrew McQuilkin, FRDI
International President
Retail Design Institute

TRY TO IMAGINE YOUR NEW LIGHTING PROJECT.
NOW, YOU MAY COME TO TRUST AND DISCOVER IT.

Please come and interact and experiment all of the effects and sensations that each lighting system offers to the public in the most diversified retail environments.

For the past 40 years, TRUST has been acting in both the development and manufacturing as well as the import and export of light fixtures and lighting systems using the most advanced technology and innovating design, always keeping in mind economy in energy and high efficiency in lighting technology. It has achieved elevated results which are tested and proven daily in its modern showroom with a brand new concept of light in several retail environments. Business space of the most diversified activities and large department stores are supplied and equipped with trust products in shopping centers and business areas all over Brazil and the Americas.

Bring your project and let TRUST work it out for you.

INTRODUCTION

On the following pages of *Stores of the Year No. 20* we are very pleased to present a beautifully photographed tour of The Retail Design Institute's International Store Design Competition accompanied by illuminating text. This armchair tour celebrates exceptional global retail design projects from over 20 categories, from full-line department stores to manufacturer's showrooms.

As time passes, things change. Retailing is no different. However, some things remain timeless: innovative store design and expert visual merchandising promote product as no website or advertisement can. The product, and the style and technology used to display it may evolve, but the bottom line remains unchanged: irresistible products and their presentation remain an oasis for shoppers.

The 37 projects presented here perfectly illustrate this and we send our congratulations to all the featured firms and the talented and dedicated people who conceived and constructed, designed and delivered, to make the experience of in-store shopping a pleasurable experience for the consumer and a profitable experience for the retailer . . . and a special congratulations to Umpqua Bank 2013's Store of the Year.

This year, RDI's Southern California Chapter hosted the judging of the Institute's 43rd Competition. The panel was comprised of industry leaders representing retailers and design firms with diverse viewpoints from strategy to trend forecasting and design, construction and anthropology. A brief bio of each participating judge appears on the "Meet the Judges" page.

The judging criteria followed the following guidelines:
Conceptual Design - the primary idea and its delivery in supporting the project
Branding - how well the design delivers on the brand promise through demonstrating strategic thinking
Store Planning - layout, overall design and customer journey
Lighting - general and special use of lighting to highlight the design and customer journey
Materiality/Finishes - overall selection of the materials and key customer touch points
Wayfinding Signage & Environmental Graphics - tie-in the brand message and design
Visual Merchandising - the display and presentation story/concept
Fixtures & Fittings - design and shop-ability
Digital Integration - i.e. e-commerce, website, mobile, kiosk, hand-held, in-store and on-line
Sustainability - sustainable concept approach, materials specification, sourcing, construction, and/or fabrication are regarded as "green," and their relationship to the brand and the customer journey

We hope that you enjoy your armchair tour and find inspiration in these outstanding examples of visual merchandising, store planning and design.

John Hogan
Editor

MEET THE JUDGES

The Retail Design Institute's International Store Design Competition celebrates exceptional global retail design projects from over 20 categories from full-line department stores to manufacturer's showrooms. This year, the Southern California Chapter stepped up to host judging of the Institute's 43rd Competition. The Judging Committee was comprised of retailers and design firms with diverse viewpoints from strategy to trend forecasting and design, construction and anthropology.

Judging Committee

James Farnell RDI, Creative Director, Little (Judging Chair)
James is a retail design specialist with over 20 years experience working in multidisciplinary design studios renowned for their creation of world-class integrated environments. While living in the Far East he was responsible for projects across the Asia Pacific region, including Dell, Proctor & Gamble, Apple, DFS and HP. Now in California at a leading architectural firm, James is responsible for Little's creative output for the Brand Experience Studio. He is a member of the RDI's International Board of Directors and is currently President of the Southern California Chapter.

Philip Otto, Principal, Otto Design Group (Judging Co-Chair)
Cultural anthropologist turned designer, Philip Otto explores the intersection between architecture, design, art, and culture. In his career he has maintained dialog between these interconnected worlds. Philip works across a variety of media to craft environments that are both practical and poetic. His client list includes Free People, Verve Coffee Roasters, Coca-Cola, Levi's, Steven Alan, Undefeated, Anthropologie and Urban Outfitters to name a few.

Judges

Giorgio Borruso FRDI, Giorgio Borruso Design
Giorgio's works have appeared in over 1,000 publications, have received over 80 International Design Awards and have become an integral part of museum collections worldwide, including the Chicago Athenaeum and the Red Dot Museum in Essen, Germany. Borruso was named Retail Design Luminary in 2006 and Designer of the Year in 2005 by DDI magazine. He is a frequent lecturer on innovation, design, and architectural theory at universities and conferences globally. Recent works include Fornari Group Offices in Milan, Carlo Pazolini in Milan/New York/Rome/London and the Snaidero USA showroom in New York.

Brian M. Dyches FRDI, Chief Experience Designer & Digital Strategist at Openeye Global
Brian is an authority on digital marketing & in-store experience. As a thought leader, he has addressed more than 30,000 leaders in civic, government, travel/hospitality and financial industries, as well as leading brands and manufacturers on five continents about the trends & methods impacting customer experience. He served as the International Chairman & President of the Retail Design Institute. Brian's global experience now serves clients of Openeye as the lead experience designer & digital strategist.

Nicole Guarascio Senior Trend Specialist, Stylesight
Nicole is an authoritative voice of the industry with her finger on the pulse of what's happening in fashion, lifestyle and design. Previously she worked at a luxury e-commerce site as business and brand manager. She has also worked for retailers American Eagle, Macy's and American Apparel as a visual merchandiser and product feedback manager. At Stylesight, Nicole ensures that her clients have a well-rounded understanding of emerging and evolutionary trends. From fashion and technology to consumer behavior, she communicates the company's trend reports in a way that is applicable to each of her clients.

Christopher Love RDI, Vice President of Architecture & Construction, BCBG Maxazria Group
Chris leads a team of professionals responsible for the global design, construction and material procurement for all 22 brands retail environments, corporate offices, trade shows/showrooms and licensees. He has been in the retail design business for over 28 years including positions with leading retail design firms Walker Group/CNI, CLDA and RKI creating and executing environments for many brands: Macy's, Bloomingdales, Harrods of London, Saks Fifth Avenue, Barneys New York, and Ralph Lauren to name a few. Presently he is an instructor at FIDM in Los Angeles and a Professional Member of the RDI.

Luanne Perry FRDI, Vice President of Design, Group 7 Design
Luanne is a creative design professional with over 25 years experience in Retail Design and Construction. Her main focus is to lead a group of designers through the development of national retail prototypes and roll out programs while nurturing existing clients as well as developing new ones. While with an independent interior design and store planning firm she has worked with Bose, Zounds Hearing, Trans World Entertainment, and others. Luanne is also a principal of the company and a member of its Board of Directors.

William Alton RDI, Director of Design, Paramount Pictures Parks and Resorts
Under William's creative direction, Paramount's Parks and Resorts Group have experienced unprecedented growth in the recreation and hospitality markets. Projects include: the Paramount Park in Murcia, Spain; the Star Fleet Recruiting Center (Star Trek) in Aqaba, Jordan; and the Paramount Hotels and Resorts chain. He supervises the creative and design development of all national and international aspects of recreation and hospitality for Paramount. Previously as senior designer for the Paramount Parks Group, he oversaw design for all new attractions, retail, and dining projects. He is a professional member of the RDI.

Kambiz Hemati RDI, Partner, L.O.V.E. Love Observed Vision Explored, Inc.
Kambiz has 20 years of agency and in-house experience. He leads design teams on multiple award winning flagships, prototypes & global roll out programs for Nike, Starbucks, BCBG, Fila and other independent retailers. As Nike's Global Creative Director of Store Design, he managed the US, EU and China teams on multiple store projects. Kambiz grew up in Switzerland and studied architecture, graphic design and film production design in Los Angeles. A member of the RDI, he recently has spoken at Global Shop, the Retail Facilities Summit, the Retail Design Forum, and the Intelligence Group. His projects have appeared in design magazines and the general media globally.

CAPTURE COUTURE

MARK STEELE PHOTOGRAPHY

photo: **PIRCH**

focused on capturing the design intent of high-end retail environments

www.marksteelephotography.com
614 291 0519

design:retail

designretailonline.com

WELCOME TO THE NEW AGE

WHAT HAPPENS WHEN DIGITAL AND RETAIL BLEND SEAMLESSLY?

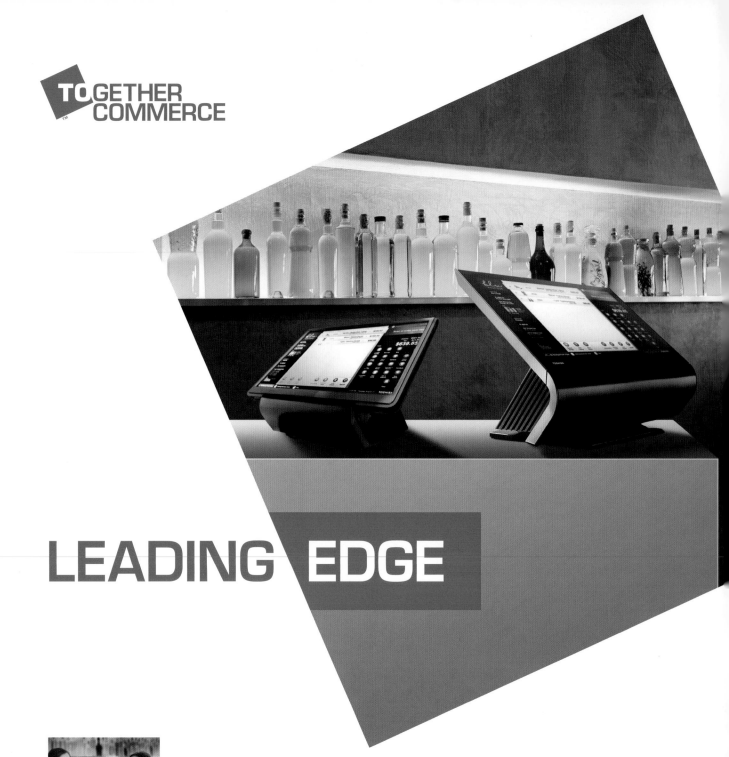

TOGETHER COMMERCE™

LEADING EDGE

After more than 20 years as a world leader in store technology, Toshiba understands the importance of design in perfecting the in-store experience. And it's not just about aesthetics. It's about designing equipment like the TCxWave™ that can withstand the rigors of a messy market – and that runs software as powerful as it is simple. It's about servicing that won't interrupt store operations and entire stores that embody a brand promise. We know design. Let's talk. toshibacommerce.com

TOSHIBA
Leading Innovation »»

STORE OF THE YEAR: **WINNER**
FINANCIAL SERVICE: **WINNER**

Umpqua Bank San Francisco

450 Sansome Street, San Francisco, CA 94111

SCOPE OF WORK

The challenge for this flagship store was to evolve Umpqua's successful neighborhood model, blending high-tech banking with dramatic presence and a high-touch environment to welcome and engage the local community. Emphasis was placed on positioning, consumer strategy and experience mapping, development of the façade and exterior signage, design of all interior elements and touch points, communication strategy, digital integration, storytelling and specification of all materials, finishes and custom elements.

GOALS AND OBJECTIVES

Major points focused upon were creating a facility that sets the tone and drives demand, communicating the brand and its relevance to both business and individual clients, drive interest by creating a "destination" and "must-see" experience, engage customers through unique amenities, service and information tools, and the use of technology to deliver the ultimate banking experience.

GOALS ACHIEVED

The exterior signage literally stops passersby, and the praise from the press and Umpqua's team have brought to fruition CEO Ray Davis' directive to make the store a "Roman candle." Further, customers and guests have used the facilities for meetings and gatherings, community events have been sold out, and many visitors have switched their banking to Umpqua.

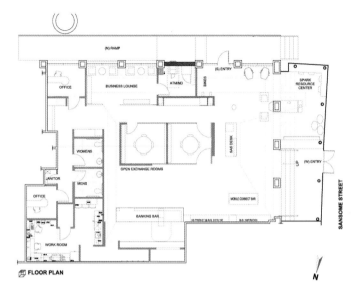

FLOOR PLAN

BRAND PROMISE

Umpqua's brand promise is to be "The World's Greatest Bank." The concierge desk, amenities in the lounge areas, refreshments, bicycles and iPads to borrow contribute to every customer feeling valued. New technology is making banking as seamless as possible. Banking associates with iPads and wireless headsets help customers anywhere in the space.

CUSTOMER JOURNEY

The customer journey has been choreographed to emphasize relationship and community building, with banking transactions accessible, but not accentuated. Dynamic signage and informational video screens draw customers closer. The façade is transparent with clear views into the space. Inside is space for learning, relaxing and surfing. The Concierge Desk is positioned and functions much as it would in a hotel.

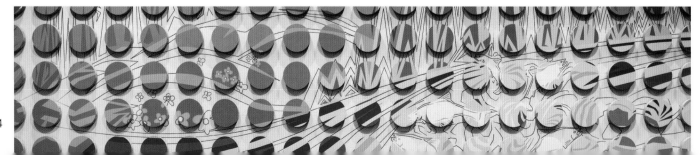

BRANDING

Branding expresses two aspects of "The World's Greatest Bank" promise: innovation and hospitality. The exterior sign, with ever-changing content projected in the Umpqua logo, ties to innovation. The reclaimed wood monument with its illuminated logo adds warmth and speaks to the hospitality that comes from Umpqua's Northwest heritage.

ENVIRONMENTAL GRAPHICS

Environmental graphics weave in themes of innovation and currency. Patterns are derived from pennies, and the notion of a whole made from many small parts. This is visible in the dot pattern used in the large mural. Interior communication integrates analog and digital branding, wayfinding, storytelling and informational content.

STORE PLANNING

Customer connection and interaction points are closest to the street or at the center of the space. The more public and social spaces give way to semi-private, private and transactional spaces as customers move through the space. A circular flow is created around the centrally located Exchange Rooms.

FIXTURING

A Local Spotlight at the front of the store features interactive content and a place for a selected local business partner to showcase their offering. The Hospitality Bar includes a merchandised end cap of artisan and proprietary coffee and tea, which are also offered as refreshment to customers in the store.

FINISHES

A concerted effort was made to make the space feel very modern, yet warm, textural and inviting. Reclaimed wood was sourced from structures with historical roots. Umpqua's signature colors were reflected in the selection of finishes, tiles, furnishings and accessories.

LIGHTING

Custom fixtures were designed for the Concierge Desk, the Banking Services Bar, and the alley window wall accentuating areas designated for customer interactions. Indirect lighting highlights various communication elements, including the large Catalyst Wall, an interactive touch screen wall. All lighting within the store is LED.

VISUAL MERCHANDISING

Umpqua is unique in the banking world in its storytelling approach. The large-scale touch screen to the right of the Local Spotlight invites customers to explore the bank's offering in the context of their personal financial journey. Financial apps are available free for customers to better manage their finances.

DESIGN FIRM
Huen, Portland, OR

PROJECT DESIGN TEAM
Craig Wollen, Principal, Creative
Director
Rebecca Huston, Principal, Strategy
Cody Barnickel, Principal,
Communication Design
Shane Fletcher, Design Director

STORE DESIGN TEAM
Lani Hayward, Executive VP,
Creative Strategies
Tomomi Marzan, VP, Design
Manager
Valarie Hamm, VP, Brand Experience
Design Director
Kate Zimmerman, Art Director

ARCHITECT
McCall Design Group, San
Francisco, CA
John Chan, Senior VP

GENERAL CONTRACTOR
Skyline Construction, San
Francisco, CA
Don MacKinnon, Superintendent

OUTSIDE DESIGN CONSULTANTS

Lighting:
Revolver Design, Berkeley, CA
Michael Webb

Graphic Production:
Forge Graphic Works, Portland, OR
Todd Ebersole

Digital Content:
Belle and Wissell, Co., Seattle, WA
Sara Faulkner

Media/Digital Engineering:
CM Salter, San Francisco, CA
Elisabeth Kelson

SUPPLIERS

Cabinetry and Millwork:
Tamalpais Cabinetry, Richmond, CA

Carpet:
Masland Carpets, Saraland, AL

Floor Tile:
Daltile, Dallas, TX

Paint:
Miller Paints, Portland, OR
Sherwin Williams, Cleveland, OH
Benjamin Moore, Montvale, NJ

Countertops:
Corian, Wilmington, DE

Furniture:
Smith CFI, Portland, OR
Inform, Seattle, WA

Custom Lighting:
Resolute Lighting, Seattle, WA

Chandeliers:
Moooi, The Netherlands

Window Coverings:
Mechosystems, Long Island City, NY

Suspended Ceiling:
USG, Chicago, IL

Reclaimed Wood:
Pioneer Millworks, McMinnville, OR

We started Huen with a simple idea: to create a place where a team of smart creative people could collaborate to do some great work.

Our business is built on understanding and developing the relationships between consumers and brands, and translating that knowledge into effective retail experiences that harness communication, environment, visual merchandising and service to drive retail success. Whether we're engaged with a globally recognized name or a newly emerging brand, we're here to turn insights into solutions that change what consumers think and do.

WHAT WE DO

STRATEGY
Brand Positioning
Go To Market Strategies
Retail Audit & Analysis
Retail Strategy
Consumer & Market Insights
Communication Platform
Experience Mapping

DESIGN
Branded & Retail Environments
Communication & Identity Design
Temporary Experiences
Brand & Product Marketing
Environmental Graphics

ACTIVATION
Design Development
Visual Merchandising
Project Management
Production Coordination
Installation Support

LEADERSHIP

REBECCA HUSTON
Principal, Strategy

CRAIG WOLLEN
Principal, Creative Director

CODY BARNICKEL
Principal, Communication Design

CARI COYER
VP, Marketing

HUEN

1911 NW Quimby Street
Portland, OR
97209

503 224 4836

huenspace.com

cari@huenspace.com

Teva

Sephora

Dick's Sporting Goods

Liverpool Veracruz El Dorado

Boca del Rio, Veracruz, Mexico

SCOPE OF WORK

The design included three primary elements: the location in front of a marina in a new residential zone, the façade and the triple high wall in the Food Hall "Experiencia Gourmet" for an extraordinary view of the marina, and the overall interior architecture and selection of materials that integrate within the space.

GOALS AND OBJECTIVES

The architectural objective was to create an elegant destination utilizing a flexible layout, Outposts in strategic locations encourage customers to explore and discover while timeless and neutral design places the focus on the merchandise. The Food Tower provides food offerings at all levels. The experience is warm, relaxed and inviting.

GOALS ACHIEVED

The new store has been designed as a social oasis for the new, upscale beach community. A place to unwind, be revived and refreshed, the sun-drenched store celebrates its natural surround-ings, acting as an artful canvas of discovery, to become a lifestyle destination connecting with the local community and its culture.

BRAND PROMISE

The new design delivers on the Liverpool message to their customer: "This is a store for me and my family," a store that becomes a public social oasis, a place that not only has a physical but an emotional reference to the community. The store becomes a true retail destination with the latest fashion, food and entertainment.

CUSTOMER JOURNEY

The "art of nature" is evoked through variation in architectural scale and form while the organic circulation leads the customer on a path of natural discovery. Sun and shadow harmoniously filter through architectural screens at the heart of the store introducing a lively pattern of movement throughout the day. Layering of lines and bending of forms simulates the motion of wind while the golden sea is reflected through materiality to create a dialogue between customer and space.

BRANDING

The store becomes a public social oasis, a place that not only has a physical but an emotional reference to the community. This is a retail destination where the latest fashion, food and exclusive entertainment experiences can be found.

PLANNING

Main aisle circulation is a simple, round flow with wide aisles that streamlines effortless movement through the store. Bold, circular detailing in the architecture allows for an organic customer journey. These circular patterns are repeated throughout on ceilings, floors and escalator wells.

FIXTURING

A space was created that balances nature and modernism. The sun-drenched store celebrates its natural surroundings while acting as an artful canvas of discovery with its modern, clean finishes.

FINISHES

A variety of texture, color, and organic shapes accomplishes the balance of nature and modernism. Movement and texture in the flooring was achieved by using a 60% to 40% ratio of marble and porcelain tile introducing the natural elements and allowing a mixture of man-made materials.

LIGHTING

The lighting supports the different designs for each room, giving a distinct atmosphere, personality and feeling to each. Natural light floods the Food Hall with a three-story wall of windows including a unique view out to the Boca del Rio marina.

VISUAL MERCHANDISING

Focus on the merchandise was created via a timeless and neutral design. An entrance was created for each department inviting the customer to enter. These entry areas are a prelude of what is yet to come, to highlight the latest trend and let the wide selection of Liverpool merchandise to do the speaking.

DESIGN FIRM
FRCH Design Worldwide,
Cincinnati, OH

PROJECT DESIGN TEAM

HeeSun Kim, VP Design Creative Director, Design Lead
Young Rok Park, VP Design, Creative Director, Design Assistant
Claudia Cerchiara, VP Client and Project Manager
Steve Gardner, VP Principal
Lara Roller, Senior Designer
Amanda Searfoss, Junior Designer
Amy Baffin, Junior Designer
Deb Casey, Senior Planner & Merchandising
Lori Kolthoff, Creative Director, Resource Design
Jennifer Eng, Senior Designer
Brad Kalchek, Senior Architect, Bim Manager
Jonathan Woodn, Senior Architect, Bim Manager
Anne Fugazi, Junior Architect
Joe Brumback, Junior Architect, Bim Manager

STORE DESIGN TEAM

Martin Perez, General Store Planning Manager
Iliana Davila, Corporate Store Planning Manager
Fernando Parrillat, Corporate IT Manager
Maria Elena Meneses, Vendor Manager
Javier Robles, Store Planning Coordinator
Jose Manuel Zurutuza, Architectural Design and Fixture Coordinator
Laura Flores, Vendor Coordinator
Carlos Jimenez, IT Coordinator
Dario Garrido, Architectural Design and Fixture Manager
Adriana Limon, Fixture Manager
Rocio Monroy, Finishes and Materials Manager
Alejandro Ruiz, Graphics and Signage Senior Manager
Francisco Partida, Overall Project

Store Manager
Enrique Norten, Ten Arquitectos (facade designer)
Alejandro Niz, Niz+Chauvet (restaurant designer)

ARCHITECT

FRCH Design Worldwide,
Cincinnati, OH

GENERAL CONTRACTOR

Liverpool Team:

Roberto Pazos, Construction Director
Jose Luis Garelli, Construction Manager
Oscar Robledo, Construction Coordinator

External Consultant:

JC Construcciones (building site coordinator)
Juan Carlos Soto

OUTSIDE DESIGN CONSULTANTS

Furniture, Perimeter and Generic Corners:

PC Proyectos
GM Vialdi
LIGHTMEX

Flooring Contractor:

Luqstones
Stones Piedras Naturales

SUPPLIERS

Structural Engineering:

Camba Y Asociados

Engineering External Consultants (Sanitary Installation):

GMG

Electrical Installation:

Enrique Margaleff

Air Conditioning Installation:

Ricardo Michel

Lord & Taylor Mizner Park

200 Plaza Real, Boca Raton, Florida 33432

SCOPE OF WORK

This project was a full takeover renovation of an 80,000 square feet abandoned furniture store that included branding the existing façade, complete store planning, and interior design.

GOALS AND OBJECTIVES

The prime objective was to create a new branded interior design position that realizes the essence of Lord & Taylor and will become the basis of other projects moving forward.

GOALS ACHIEVED

The new, layered design has contributed to the store operating well ahead of revenue plans. The key design elements are being retrofitted into existing projects and as the basis for new locations.

BRAND PROMISE

Lord & Taylor aims to offer an upscale experience but not exclusively upscale merchandise. Maintaining the upscale shopping experience was paramount; "We don't want our stores to be too crowded or cluttered. It's all part of the elevated shopping experience," says Rodbell, President of Lord & Taylor. "We spend a lot of time on directionals for visual presentation and work closely with the execution of visuals." Great customer service is key. "We have coaching programs in place because we're really focused on our selling team being consumer-centric," concludes Rodbell.

CUSTOMER JOURNEY

Transitioning from the open-air pedestrian mall, there are three approaches into the store: the celebrated, portico'd center aisle main entrance, and two corner entrances. The guest transitions from the Mizner-inspired center that builds into American-Classic architecture with Boca-inspired wood ceilings that guide the guest throughout the main aisle. A classic architectural transition between the worlds becomes the backdrop to visual trend zones. Fitting room and services portals also speak to the key attributes of the brand. Service and cash desks are within each of the sub-departments, convenient to the guest and department sales associates.

BRANDING

Branding celebrates the high-end services and amenities through architecture and fine finishes, but is simple and modern enough to speak to middle- and upper-middle class guests.

ENVIRONMENTAL GRAPHICS

Wayfinding has been relegated within the architecture for amenities and services and kept minimal.

STORE PLANNING

The two biggest challenges were the corner entrances and the existing position of the escalators. Entrances: Oval foyer forms were used to ease the guest into the Richter linear store planning. Escalators: the existing escalators, which remain, faced the old abandoned entrance. The entrance was converted to a show window open to the selling floor leveraging the phototropism of natural light to help cue the guest to the vertical circulation.

FIXTURING

Modern polished chrome and white lacquer fixturing with hints of a Floridian sun-bleached wood became the "fashion" layer to complement the trends and fashions of Lord & Taylor.

FINISHES

The team selected the whitest porcelain floors and lacquered columns to note the heritage of the Lord & Taylor brand, with hints of Boca Raton through mosaics and the beach wood ceilings.

LIGHTING

A knife-edge, whole lit, floating slab illuminates the bleached wood ceilings as an aid to wayfinding navigation. With the introduction of over 300 mannequins and visual moments, accent lighting became an important drama-making layer.

VISUAL MERCHANDISING

The magical layer added in coordination during the store planning process with Lord & Taylor's visual department is comprised of over 300 mannequins and 50 major moments within the store.

DESIGN FIRM
BHDP Architecture,
Cincinnati, OH

PROJECT DESIGN TEAM
BHDP Architecture, Cincinnati, OH

ARCHITECT
BHDP Architecture, Cincinnati, OH

GENERAL CONTRACTOR
Turner Construction, Miami, FL

SUPPLIERS
All Modern Lighting, Boston, MA
Amitco Vinyl, Atlanta, GA
Andreu World USA Furniture, Cincinnati, OH
Arcadia Contract Furniture, La Palma, CA
ARC COM, Orangeburg, NY
Architectural Systems, Inc., New York, NY
Architex Fabric, Northbrook, IL
Armstrong Vinyl, Lancaster, PA
Arte for Koroseal Wall Covering/ RJF Intl Corp., Fairlawn, OH
Atlas Carpet, Los Angeles, CA
Atlas Concorde Tile, Cincinnati, OH
ASI, New York, NY
Benjamin Moore Paint, Montvale, NJ
Bevara Design House Furniture, San Rafael, CA
Brueton, Freeport, NY
Cape Contract Furniture, Cincinnati, OH
Carnegie Wall Covering Fabric, Cincinnati, OH
Cumberland, Grand Rapids, MI
Design Tex, Blue Ash, OH
Design Within Reach, Stamford, CT

Dupont Zodiaq Solid, Cincinnati, OH
Elitis Wall Covering, Beachwood, OH
Euro Style Lighting, Porter Ranch, CA
Fadini Borghi Fabric, Beachwood, OH
Gus Design Group, Inc., Cincinnati, OH
Indiana Furniture, Lewis Center, OH
Interface Flor Carpet Tile, Lagrange, GA
JPMA Metal, Montreal, QC Canada
Knoll Fabric, Cincinnati, OH
Lumens Lighting, Sacramento, CA
Luxo, Florence, KY
Maharam Fabric, Hauppauge, NY
Mannington Commercial, Columbus, OH
Marset Lighting, New York, NY
Miliken Carpet, Spartanburg, SC
Nora Wood Flooring, Forest, VA
Parterre Vinyl, Cincinnati, OH
Phillip Jeffries, Ltd., Fairfield, NJ
Plaskolite, Inc. Acrylic, Columbus, OH
Pollack Fabric, Beachwood, OH
Reid Witlin, Ltd. Fabric, Cincinnati, OH
Renolit Covaren Plastic Laminate, Swedesboro, NJ
RJE Business Interiors Furniture, Cincinnati, OH
Rytel Holland Contract Furniture, Cincinnati, OH
Shaw Contract Group Carpet Tile, Cincinnati, OH
Sondra Alexander RJF Intl Corp., Fairlawn, OH
Stone Source Tile Mosaic Stone, New York, NY
Stone Tile Wood Flooring, Toronto, ON Canada
The Tile Shop, Florence, KY
Quick Step, Dallas, TX

BHDP

Design for **People**

We design environments
that affect the key behaviors
necessary to achieve strategic
results for our clients

www.bhdp.com

Barneys New York

660 Madison Avenue, New York, NY 10065

SCOPE OF WORK

The project included the complete redesign of select departments and master planning within those departments. The first phase included the women's jewelry and accessories on the main level and a full-floor shoe department containing men's and women's merchandise and accessories. The second phase comprised the men's accessories on the main level.

GOALS AND OBJECTIVES

To present the merchandise first and foremost it was imperative to bring the focus directly to the product. A big and noteworthy change was necessary to re-energize the store, and reinforce it's positioning in the New York market as an iconic shopping institution, as well as an international shopping destination.

GOALS ACHIEVED

The ground floor experience sets the tone for the entire store. Open vistas are maintained through organized planning of specific sub-departments and the restrained use of materials are thoughtful and clear. Important elements such as light, organization and overall retail appeal were strongly considered in the new design, based on the inherent forms rather than decoration. This approach sets the tone for the store's new image. Custom displays incorporate clear glass boxes perched on rectilinear boxes clad in a light European Oak veneer. Glass shelves seemingly float off Calcutta marble slab walls—all designed to add emphasis to the products on a minimalist backdrop.

BRAND PROMISE

Positioned at the top end of retail and fashion, Barneys endeavors to provide shoppers with a curated shopping experience that delights and engages shoppers. An iconic New York institution and international shopping destination, Barneys presents their point of view with taste, luxury and humor.

CUSTOMER JOURNEY

In the new shoe department, and on the main level, the division between categories is blurred. Shoppers flow from one area to another effortlessly supporting the way merchandise is curated on the selling floor. The seamless integration of men's and women's departments and a gender neutral palette results in a comfortable shopping environment for both. Opened up as much as possible, low central display fixtures along central corridors maintain open views to all angles of the floor.

BRANDING

The design is presented with confidence and authority, reaffirming Barneys' position as a New York institution, and within the global marketplace.

STORE PLANNING

Open sightlines, and the seamless transition between departments encourages shoppers to flow from one area to the next and supports the way the merchandise is curated on the selling floor. Gender neutrality of the design allows for seamless integration and cross-over

of men's and women's departments, and also means an accessible, comfortable environment for both sexes.

FIXTURING

Merchandise presentation is the primary focus. The sophisticated detailing of this Fixturing Innovation Award winner brings the product to the forefront, be it in the form of cantilevered shelves that fade into the background when an incredible bag is perched upon them, or intricately engineered glass fixturing that allows for an unobstructed view of the merchandise.

FINISHES

The new design concept places an emphasis on materials setting a minimalist tone for the entire store. Calcutta marble slabs, glass and European oak are used throughout. Custom carpets and soft furnishings on the shoe floor add warmth and texture.

LIGHTING

Ambient lighting from back-lit panels, wall niches and coves paired with directional lighting and integrated fixture lighting all work together to create a warm, welcoming ambience and highlight the merchandise.

VISUAL MERCHANDISING

The interior design concept supports the way the merchandise is presented, allowing opportunities for the Barneys visual merchandising team to work freely. Long, low display fixtures provide the opportunity to display merchandise in a fresh, interesting way.

DESIGN FIRM
Yabu Pushelberg,
New York, NY

PROJECT DESIGN TEAM
Yabu Pushelberg
George Yabu
Glenn Pushelberg

Phase 1:
Cherie Stinson
Carrie Stinson
Samer Shaath
Enrique Mangalindan

Phase 2:
Rise Endo
Lizette Viloria
Yuki Kubota
Jessica Shaw
Joe Kim
Matthew Bradshaw
Steffi Min

STORE DESIGN TEAM
Philippe WY Hum, Sr VP Store
Design & Construction

ARCHITECT
Lalire March Architects, New York, NY

GENERAL CONTRACTOR
Shawmut Design & Construction,
New York, NY

OUTSIDE DESIGN CONSULTANTS
Lighting Consultant:
Cooley Monato, New York, NY
Emily Monato, Andressa Lopes

Stair Consultant:
Jaroff Design, Hicksville, NY
Joe Jaroff

SUPPLIERS
Sourced and supplied by the client

Lane Crawford Yintai

Yintai Centre, 2, Jianguomenwai Street, Chaoyang District, Beijing

SCOPE OF WORK

Located in the Yintai Centre in Beijing, a multi-use complex that also houses the Park Hyatt Beijing, Park Hyatt Residences, offices, and shopping, this new Lane Crawford is the brand's smallest, most intimate store conceived to cater to a select clientele. The scope of work included the complete planning and design of the entire store.

GOALS AND OBJECTIVES

Lane Crawford Yintai was designed with one customer in mind. The brand's second highest spender had requested a store for her and her friends. Yintai was the response to that request. The goal was to create an intimate shopping experience that caters to the needs of one very important customer, and speaks to her aesthetic and philosophy.

GOALS ACHIEVED

Open to the public by appointment, and catering mainly to VIPs, this store has a highly curated product mix based on the aesthetics and philosophy of the customer. The overall design is intimate and engaging, a collection of rooms reminiscent of a private apartment or mansion with different rooms evoking different moods and experiences. Compartmentalized spaces, freestanding fixtures and custom finishes support the exclusive feeling.

CUSTOMER JOURNEY

The journey through the store provides a well-choreographed sense of discovery. The offering is highly focused and curated to reflect the desires and needs of visiting VIPs, and the design supports that.

BRANDING

The DNA of the Lane Crawford brand is captured, building on an existing vocabulary, and evolving the conversation for this location. The design has art woven through, and the concept overall is edited and pared back. A conscience effort was made to edit the design to reflect the brand and designer's collective vision of the mood of where luxury design is headed.

STORE PLANNING

Linked rooms produce interesting sightlines and vistas; visual cues and special treatments draw visitors through the interconnected spaces. Rooms are intimate in scale, flowing from one to another. Utilizing full-height pivoting doors and screens, each room can be closed and compartmentalized from the rest, in effect creating a private chamber, or giant fitting room. A small selection of menswear is housed in similarly intimate quarters on the mezzanine level, accessed by elevator or via the grand staircase.

FIXTURING

The fixtures are all freestanding so they can be changed, moved and reconfigured, like furniture. This store also allows for more open space. Because the merchandise is selected and curated to appeal to the specific taste of VIPs, there was less pressure to fill every linear foot with merchandise. The imprint of merchandise is more rarefied and unique, encapsulating limited run products and the like and allowing the display of art.

FINISHES

Many special finishes are used that are artistic in form and feeling, and integrate into the interior design in this Materiality/Finishes Innovation Award winner. Art elevates the work; commissioned art and custom finishes clearly differentiate this store from any other. Walls are mounted with back-lit, gesso-ed artist's canvasses painted to imply interior detailing, sconces, paneling, etc.

LIGHTING

All the rooms within the store glow. Wall-mounted white artists canvasses are back-lit, diffusing light, and creating a halo effect behind the merchandise.

VISUAL MERCHANDISING

Lane Crawford prides itself as one of the best editors of product and best visual merchandisers in the world. Their teams excel at creating change within the store environment so in some areas somewhat recessive design is created to support the ever-evolving installations.

DESIGN FIRM
Yabu Pushelberg, Toronto, ON
Canada

PROJECT DESIGN TEAM
George Yabu
Glenn Pushelberg
Mary Mark
Eduardo Figueredo
Tracy Morton
Chun Yiu Lam
Eiri Ota
Sunny Leung
Janis Yung
Chris French
Chris Chen

ARCHITECT
Linea Partnership LLP, Beijing, China
Eric Jung

OUTSIDE DESIGN CONSULTANTS
Lighting Designer:
Inverse Lighting Design Ltd., London, UK
Filip Vermeiren

SUPPLIERS
Carpets:
Creative Matters Inc., Toronto, ON Canada

DFS Galleria, Scottswalk

25 Scotts Road, Singapore 228220

SCOPE OF WORK

DFS Galleria Scottswalk was a complete renovation from the core structure out of the ground and first floors and minor adjustments on the second and third floors. Beauty was relocated from the first to ground floor and luxury categories from ground floor to first. A completely new façade is underway with visual openings into retail and the 6m height of the ground floor.

GOALS AND OBJECTIVES

Within the completely renovated areas the clear objective was to create a new global benchmark of DFS Galleria retail planning, brand integration to the benefit of all, design, materials, visual merchandising, event and customer service amenities.

GOALS ACHIEVED

The objective of creating a new global benchmark was spectacularly achieved in the entirely renovated areas of the first and ground floors successfully integrating the brand into the design, materials, event/customer service amenities and visual merchandising.

BRAND PROMISE

The completed renovation presents the ultimate in luxury accessibility and emersion with best in class customer service and amenities across all specialty categories presented within an environment both beneficial to the customer and retailer.

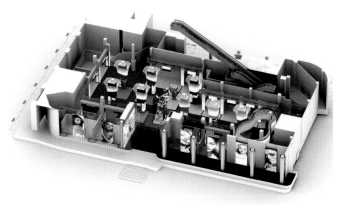

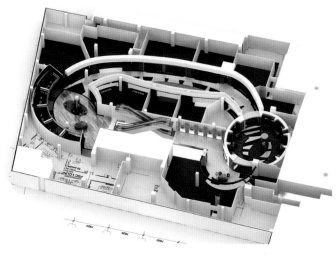

CUSTOMER JOURNEY

The conducted tour customer visits the entire store on a proposed flow within a defined time frame while independent customers flow as they will. VIP customers access best in class amenities like platinum services lounges with private rooms, make up rooms, kitchen and business center facilities. Personal shoppers present customer selected merchandise in the privacy of their living rooms within the PSC lounge. Beauty concierge accesses all beauty brands within a private space for treatment and color applications.

BRANDING

DFS Galleria delivers unparalleled ultimate luxury merchandise with best in class customer service and amenities and views branding as the takeaway of the retail experience over signage. The retail plan, environment, product brands, customer service and amenities all combine to deliver a unique DSF Galleria brand proposition.

ENVIRONMENTAL GRAPHICS

A dramatic feature sculpture of "falling leaves" supports an apparently random array of LED panels communicating beauty messages above the feature event space. The role of brand signage for this project was essentially brand implementation location, size and manner consistency.

STORE PLANNING

Open vistas to all beauty brand offers within the dramatic architecture of the linear ground floor are anchored at both ends with an organically shaped fragrance department. Opposite, beauty concierge creates a service destination. First floor circulation is more a specific procession of categories and brand offers along an evolving connection of rooms and a corridor spine.

FIXTURING

Two make-up stations, and fragrance and beauty brand promotion fixtures of multi level internally illuminated and trimmed in bright chrome welcome customers. Watch event space consists of a collection of reflective "jewel boxes." Vitrine Exclusive areas such as Beauty Concierge and Platinum Services Lounge are environments of comfort, personalization and service. DFS Galleria's own fixturing is primarily focused on key category and VM statements.

FINISHES

Flooring: Ground floor, reflective monotone ceramic tiles with mirror particle flecks in neutral grey frame each brand's personalized flooring. First floor, luxurious marbles of high contrasting value and veining were combined into dramatic linear patterns. Walls: ground floor, cast GRC in organic forms with almond shape perforations, multi layers of glass in translucent patterns and internal illumination create the drama of neutrality to frame each of the beauty brands. First floor, artisan shaped matte wall mosaic tiles framed in reflective dark metal provide the framework to separate brand implementation Metal: Rich combinations of reflective and matte surfaces in multiple tones of bronze support the luxury position of watches and accessories.

LIGHTING

Following a DFS self challenged LEED certification requirement, the resulting project received gold certification through the use of LED and CDMT light specification.

VISUAL MERCHANDISING

DFS Galleria visual merchandising communicates their global programs as well as local seasonal events.

DESIGN FIRM
rkd retail/iQ, Bangkok, Thailand

PROJECT DESIGN TEAM
RKurt Durrant, Principal in charge
Warisa Laingchaikul, Creative Director
Rungroj Chinbumchorn, Creative Director
Thapanee Chirathitapa, Interior Designer
Sarawut Chiracharoenchit, Senior Graphic Designer
Suphakeat Phongsuttisombat, Head of DDI
Thawatchai Tiemjarat, Head CG/3D

STORE DESIGN TEAM
Tim DeLessio, President Group East
Craig McKenna, Managing Director, South Asia
Linda Krueger, VP Worldwide Store Development
Kevin Tranbarger, VP, Business Development

Karen Taylor, Director Store Development, South Asia
Graeme Fowler, VP, Global Visual Merchandising
Perter Nauh, Director VM, South Asia

ARCHITECT
TID Associate PTE Ltd, Singapore
Lionel Ong

GENERAL CONTRACTOR
Vaford, Hong Kong
Conway Wong

OUTSIDE DESIGN CONSULTANTS
Lighting:
Iguzzini, Hong Kong
Richard Leung

CHANEL at Macy's Herald Square

Macy's Herald Square, 151 W 34th Street, New York, NY 10001

SCOPE OF WORK

In a 750 square foot space in the newly renovated Macy's Herald Square counter, CHANEL has created its latest flagship embodying its newest design codes and technological and material innovations. The space highlights the three main axis signature of CHANEL beauty: its signature makeup, skincare and fragrance consultation experiences.

GOALS AND OBJECTIVES

CHANEL sought to transform a challenging site with no backwall identity and a visually cacophonous environment into a unique expression of the brand identity. The store had to be viscerally familiar and express the firm's legacy by adapting the brand's icons while raising the sense of detail, material and craftsmanship for which CHANEL is known.

GOALS ACHIEVED

A uniquely CHANEL experience was created. A canopy is suspended by minimal glass supports and embeds an illuminated logo visible from all angles. The "walls" are translucent panes of textured glass, displaying product. The interior space is laid out with dynamic angles to create interactive experiences, provide consultations and display visuals.

BRAND PROMISE

The brand promise is to provide a unique experience that "only CHANEL can do," highlighting the firm's point of difference, from exquisite products to incredible Brand moments. Success for CHANEL is being the balance of long-term brand building and near-term business results—the equilibrium of image and commerce.

CUSTOMER JOURNEY

A dynamic walk-in environment enhances the presentation of the products. The overhead CC logo is a main focal point. Mirroir Lumieres are hallmarks of makeup expertise with tailored lighting. The LED screen is a beacon seen from the new Macy's "Memorial" Entrance. Innovative Makeup displays provide artful presentation of iconic packaging.

BRANDING

CHANEL had a challenging site with no backwall identity and a visually discordant environment. These obstacles were not only overcome but was declared a Branding Innovation Award winner when a new yet viscerally familiar expression of its legacy was created by inventively adapting its icons while heightening the sense of detail, material and craftsmanship for which CHANEL is known.

ENVIRONMENTAL GRAPHICS

The giant CC logo imbedded in the canopy is the focal point from the mezzanine and when inside the space. The large LED screen serves as a beacon from the newly reopened Macy's "Memorial Entrance" off 34th Street. Visible from the street, it showcases CHANEL's presence in the store.

STORE PLANNING

The layout of the counter is based off 30 and 60 degree approaches, which enhances the counter's visibility from many directions, from both the aisles and afar, instead of views found utilizing classic orthagonal schemes. Consequently, the customer is invited to engage the counter in a multitude of directions and experiences.

FIXTURING

Fixtures are both aesthetically interesting and functionally superior. Displays are elevated off the floor and constructed of textured glass as expressions of lightness and modernity. The heavily stocked displays that once served only the purpose of selling, have been elevated to works of art.

FINISHES

CHANEL continues to transcend convention and reinvent chic, as the counter reinterprets the firm's unmistakable icons. Thus, the brand colors of black, white and gold, reference of tweed and fabric in the glass, carbon fiber and tile, as well as different expressions of the CC logo, provide instantaneous brand recognition for CHANEL.

LIGHTING

Specially designed lighting elements within the canopy and fixtures enhance product presentation and provide brand identity. Mirroir Lumieres (lighted mirrors) are the hallmark of CHANEL's makeup expertise and are featured prominently, providing the most accurate makeovers tailored to lighting conditions suited to the client's locale (office, candlelight, outdoor, etc.).

VISUAL MERCHANDISING

Permanent institutional elements highlight a stronger point of view of the brand and its heritage together with ephemeral campaign elements conveying newness in conjunction with product launches. This new philosophy mixes permanent and ephemeral elements to find harmony within the context of campaign environment vs. permanent niches.

SALES TECHNOLOGY

The storefront LED wall is one of the first ultra high-resolution, high-brightness displays used in a retail application in the U.S. It utilizes a 2.5mm pixel pitch 3-in-1 SMD high contrast black LED allowing over 380 trillion colors at a viewing angle of 120° horizontal and vertical.

DESIGN
Chanel, Inc., New York, NY

PROJECT DESIGN TEAM
Chanel Design Team, New York, NY

ARCHITECT
T-Square Design Consultants, New Rochelle, NY

GENERAL CONTRACTOR
Structure Tone, Inc., New York, NY

OUTSIDE DESIGN CONSULTANTS
Lighting:
Invisible Circus, North Blenheim, NY
Structural:
Thornton Tomasetti, Newark, NJ
Electrical:
Henderson Engineers, Inc., Iselin, NJ

SUPPLIERS
Millwork:
Array (Store Fixturing Division), Bradford, ON Canada

Audio/Visual:
Ovation In-Store, Maspeth, NY
Displays:
D3, LLC, Melville, NY
Design Compendium, Brooklyn, NY
Print:
Charles Samples Peeq Media, Long Island City, NY
Flooring:
Storefloors, Atlanta, GA

RH Boston

234 Berkeley Street, Boston, Massachusetts 02116

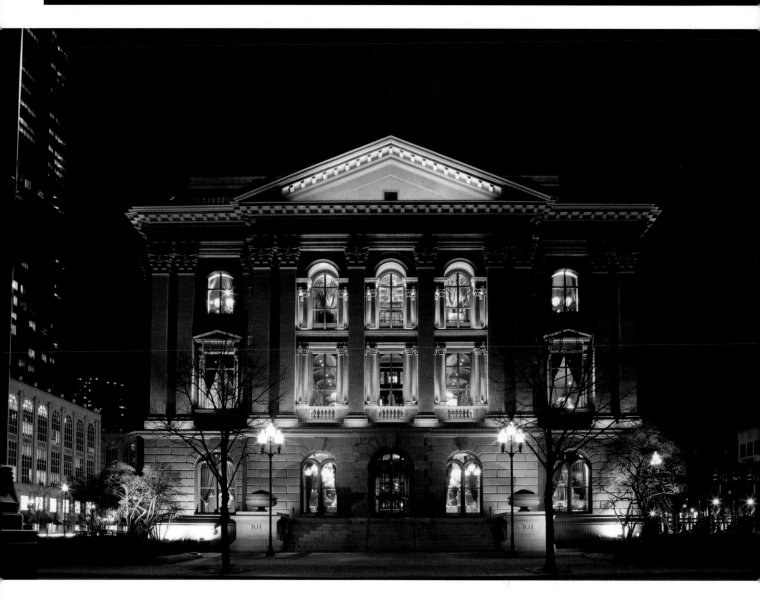

SCOPE OF WORK

The former Museum of Natural History that opened in 1863 has provided RH a venue for executing their vision of creating an immersive environment showcasing their luxury lifestyle brand in Boston's most iconic shopping destination. The grand interior of the former museum and exquisite product installations provide customers with endless design inspiration and unparalleled shopping experiences.

GOALS AND OBJECTIVES

Beyond simply creating a place to sell furniture, the project goals included providing an inspirational environment reflective of the essence of the brand. The team strove to create a transformative experience for visitors through careful attention to detail, curated product selection, and a marriage of modern and historic elements.

GOALS ACHIEVED

Bold architectural moves, such as opening up a three story central atrium anchored by a custom glass and steel traction elevator as well as connecting the building to the retail pedestrian traffic of Newbury Street through a new entry pavilion, set the stage for stunning visual merchandising.

BRAND PROMISE

The complete evolution from a traditional hardware retailer to a lifestyle brand are expressly evident in the architectural simplicity, restraint, and celebration of historic elements, and the creation of dramatic museum-scaled vignettes communicating the brand's perspective on the importance of a life filled with balance, symmetry, and proportion.

CUSTOMER JOURNEY

The opportunity to own distinctive pieces of the RH lifestyle is offered through the experience of browsing the installations of product categories such as furniture, tabletop, Baby and Child, and objects of curiosity, guided by a trained RH design associate with the brand's full catalog of offerings at their fingertips.

BRANDING

The store design allows RH the flexibility to meet their customer's specific needs of this luxury brand today while continuing to expand its brand offerings to fully outfit future needs. By locating their Boston flagship in this historic building, RH cemented their brand's commitment to harmonizing tradition with modernity.

STORE PLANNING

The store was the Innovation Award: Store Planning winner for its design solutions for intuitive circumambulation of the retail floors and galleries, each floor housing specific product categories such as Baby and Child, Dining, Outdoor, Bedroom, and Entertainment. Each gallery exudes a unique personality encouraging the customer to interact with the product in new and unexpected ways.

FIXTURING

RH was able to eliminate the need for traditional retail fixtures by showcasing product through artistic vignettes. Smaller items, such as linens and tableware, are displayed in use rather than en masse as part of a cash and carry model. Design associates work with customers to explore customization and facilitate ordering.

FINISHES

A restrained architectural material palette of plaster, glass, steel, and concrete finished in slate gray and weathered black tones provides a serene backdrop with the same core elements as the product collections. This allows unique elements, such as the gilded original coffered 70 foot tall ceiling, to capture the eye.

LIGHTING

RH's lighting product, including sconces, chandeliers, and lamps as well as ambient lighting are integral components of the vignettes throughout the store and are augmented by strategically placed track and recessed lighting highlighting specific product and architectural elements. Dramatic exterior lighting highlights the rich detailing of this historic building.

VISUAL MERCHANDISING

Unique stories are told in each gallery through the curated collection of RH product and objects of curiosity. For example, four distinctively designed clubrooms are accessed through the Parisian Garden on the third level, beckoning the customers to be transported into different worlds inspired by the RH brand.

SUSTAINABILITY

Reclaiming an historic structure that required significant structural, envelope, and infrastructure upgrades to extend its life exemplifies sustainable design thinking. Energy efficient windows matching historic profiles, new energy efficient HVAC systems and lighting controls were installed.

SALES TECHNOLOGY

Within this historic property, digital integration is seamlessly woven throughout the customer experience. The brand expression through the store, catalog, and web are consistently executed, and a team of trained design associates is available to all customers to personalize their journey via all available shopping channels.

DESIGN FIRM
Bergmeyer Associates, Inc.,
Boston, MA

DESIGN ARCHITECT
Backen Gilliam Kroeger Architect,
Sausalito CA

PROJECT DESIGN TEAM
Bergmeyer Associates, Inc.
Joseph P. Nevin, Jr., Senior Principal
Rachel J. Zsembery, Senior Associate
T.J. DiFeo, Project Manager
Backen Gilliam Kroeger Architects
Jim Gillam, Principal

ARCHITECT
Architects of Record:
Bergmeyer Associates, Inc.,
Boston, MA
Rachel J. Zsembery, AIA, LEED, AP
BD+C

Design Architects:
Backen Gilliam Kroeger Architects,
Sausalito, CA
Jim Gilliam

GENERAL CONTRACTOR
Trainor Commercial Construction,
San Rafael, CA
Brian Trainor

OUTSIDE DESIGN CONSULTANTS

Exterior Lighting:
Ross De Alessi Lighting Design,
Seattle, WA
Ross De Alessi

Interior Lighting:
Bentley Meeker, New York, NY
Bentley Meeker

Structural Engineers:
McNamara/Salvia Inc., Boston, MA
John Matuszewski

M/E/P/FP Engineers:
RW Sullivan Engineering, Boston, MA
Steven O'Connell

Landscape Architects:
Copley Wolff Design Group, Boston,
MA
Lynn Wolff

Accessibility Consultant:
Kessler McGuinness & Associates,
West Newton, MA
Katherine McGuinness

Building Enclosure Consultant:
Simpson Gumpertz & Heger,
Waltham, MA
Mark LaBonte, PE

Photographers:
Kathryn Barnard, exterior, 2nd & 3rd
floor
Jared Kuzia, staircase, Newbury
pavilion
RH, baby & child photos

SUPPLIERS

*Flooring: Soft Surface (carpeting):
Rugs; Task Lighting; Floor/table
Lamps; Pendants/Chandeliers;
Sconces; Exterior Lighting; Restroom
Faucets; Millwork at Team Break
Room; Paint Finishes/Interior Wall and*

*Trim Paint; Wallcoverings; Fabric
Finishes; Signing/Graphics:*
RH, Corte Madera, CA

Ceiling Systems: Drywall Install:
Clifford and Galvin Contracting, LLC,
West Bridgewater, MA

Lighting: Recessed lighting:
Iris Lighting Cooper Industries,
Cleveland, OH

Track Lighting:
Juno Lighting, Des Plaines, IL

Fluorescent:
Linear Lighting, Long Island City, NY
Elliptipar, West Haven, CT
GE, Fairfield, CT

*Floor/table lamps; Pendants/
Chandeliers; Sconces; Exterior
Lighting:*
GE, Fairfield, CT

IO LED Lighting:
Cooper Industries, Cleveland, OH
Elliptipar, West Haven, CT
B-K Lighting, Madera, CA

Fixtures:
Majority of fixtures provided by **RH**

Door Hardware:
Rocky Mountain Hardware, Hailey, ID
**Schlage Ingersoll Rand Security
Technologies Security and Safety
Consultants,** Needham Heights, MA

Exterior Doors Fabrication:
Sunrise Erectors Incorporated,
Canton, MA

Interior Hollow Metal Doors:
Black Mountain Door, Mt. Sterling, KY

Other Restroom Fixtures:
Toto, Morrow, GA
Elkay, Oak Brook, IL

Furniture:
Wood Connection, Inc., Modesto, CA

Misc. Trim:
Trainor Commercial Construction,
San Rafael, CA

Wall Trim:
Clifford and Galvin Contracting LLC,
West Bridgewater, MA

Interior and Exterior Metal:
Benjamin Moore, Montvale, NJ

*Metals, Glass & Special Finishes
(architectural glass/glazing / glazing
systems at winder stair, elevator and
Newbury St. entry structure):*
Sunrise Erectors Incorporated,
Canton, MA

Sound Systems:
**Bose System designed by DMX &
Mood Media,** Austin, TX

*Masonry Wall: Existing, Interior
Restoration:*
Commercial Masonry Corporation,
Plymouth, MA

Plaster Restoration and Re-creation:
Austin Ornamental, Dedham, MA

BACKEN
GILLAM
KROEGER
architects

www.bgarch.com

Left: Ram's Gate Winery/by Erhard Pfeiffer. Above: Ram's Gate Winery/by Erhard Pfeiffer, Catch Restaurant at Casa Del Mar/by Erhard Pfeiffer, Napa Valley Residence/by Erhard Pfeiffer, RH Houston Gallery/by Katheryn Barnard.

Sunglass Hut Sydney Flagship

413 George Street, Sydney, 2000, Australia

SCOPE OF WORK

The brief was to create a visionary brand statement with Asia Pacific's first, and the world's largest, Sunglass Hut Global Flagship Store.

GOALS AND OBJECTIVES

Located in the most fashionable retail area of Sydney, the Sydney Flagship, as with all flagship stores, was to be a unique and elevated expression of the Sunglass Hut brand. It had to redefine the brand experience and be location specific, and meld the DNA of Sunglass Hut, with the globally recognizable elements of Sydney: sun, beach and waves.

GOALS ACHIEVED

The design was inspired by the loop of a wave and the light reflecting from it, a reference that begins with the circular cross section of the store, and becomes increasingly evident in the Wave Room, where a high-definition print reproduces a classic wave breaking on a film that covers the whole wall, floor and ceiling. Light took on a number of interesting forms; from the sparkling floor to ceiling Lens Chandelier to the Glassiled Wall, with its 750 LEDs disappearing into infinity, and the Traxon Display in the central shopfront window, morphing light as an octopus does adapting to its surroundings.

BRAND PROMISE

The branding proves to be exceedingly effective and successful evoking adjectival expressions such as cool, savvy, sexy, fun, real and inspiring.

CUSTOMER JOURNEY

"Discover Your Cool": this concept continually evolves with ever-changing fashion and the latest style trends. The Flagship environment offers a layered experience that inspires and allows for change. It's a fluid customer journey that can take many paths and further encourages the customer to explore and discover the most current sun eyewear. The Sunglass Hut point of view is communicated by providing fashion statements, and highlighting featured brands at various focal points throughout the store.

BRANDING

The Sydney Flagship delivers on its brand promise of being an exciting and fun place to select the very latest fashion forward sunglasses. The Flagship is a clear and credible, larger-than-life expression of the Sunglass Hut brand. The elevated expression of the brand is brought about by the inclusion of only high-end materials used in its construction; from the monolithic solid surface wall displays

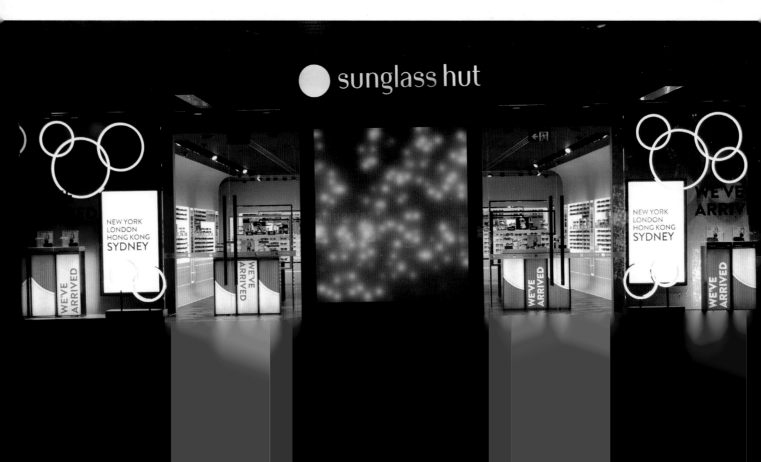

and the swirling Italian porcelain floor tiles, to the local Spotted Gum timber adorning the Luxury Room's floor, walls and ceiling.

ENVIRONMENTAL GRAPHICS

The main signs used in the Flagship are ultra-thin 22 mm (0.86") thick. The signs' composition is of a light emitting acrylic with a color-back glass panel that is masked out which is concealed glue fixed to its front panel. The result is a very low power, low maintenance, high intensity sign. This store was presented the Innovation Award: Digital Integration.

STORE PLANNING

Planning principles reflect the four phases of the customer journey: attract, discover, decide and celebrate. Gentle morphing of colors in shopfront Traxon Display garners attention from a distance, the towering Lens Chandelier provides an exciting hub to the Discovery Area, and the Glassiled Wall affords interest at the Celebration Area.

FIXTURING

All fixtures in the Flagship utilize light emitting acrylic panels (LEAP) to provide illumination. Innovative design permits their integration into the thin mirror/cupboard door, which is a LEAP panel bonded to a mirror that has been masked out at the edges allowing the panel light through.

FINISHES

The monolithic display walls were created using satin finished Staron solid surface material that allowed the curve of the wave theme to be created in a continuous form. The Luxury Room was constructed from satin finished local hardwood that was curved and laid throughout the floor, walls and ceiling.

LIGHTING

The center shopfront features a Traxon Wall generating bands of light that swirl and morph continually changing patterns. Internally, the Glassiled wall at the rear has 750 invisibly powered LEDs suspended in two sheets of glass creating an amazing infinity effect, as each LED disappears into the distance.

VISUAL MERCHANDISING

The visual merchandising calls out the multitude of brands the Flagship displays with 6"x2.8"x1" clear acrylic brand blocks. Smaller 2"x1"x1" clear acrylic blocks identify "Exclusive" and "New" released stock. Further highlighting is achieved using patterned vinyl strips to tie an area together.

SUSTAINABILITY

Staron solid surface materials can be recycled at the end of their life, and re-finished indefinitely during it, to refresh the store's presentation. All retail lighting is the latest low power LED. All timber is sourced locally from sustainable plantations and the chandelier lenses are recycled.

SALES TECHNOLOGY

The Lens Chandelier display table includes two iPads connected to the Sunglass Hut online store. Customers can use augmented reality and photograph themselves and virtually try all the latest frames. They can also choose to order and buy online from within the shop.

DESIGN FIRM
Luxottica Retail Australia
Design & Construct,
NSW, Australia

PROJECT DESIGN TEAM
Retail Sun and Luxury, Luxottica Corporate, Italy
Barbara Sani, Global Store Design Manager
Jeffrey Fisher, Global Store Experience Director, Marketing Luxottica Australia
Michael Cramp, Design and Construction Manager
Ben Mundy, Store Experience and VM Manager

STORE DESIGN TEAM
Luxottica, Australia
Alex Kessell, Luxury/Premium Buyer Sunglasses
Kellie Donaghy, Senior Planner
Cassandra Gersbach, State Sales Manager NSW

ARCHITECT
Macro Rivolta, Milan, Italy

GENERAL CONTRACTOR
McCredie Group Pty Ltd, Sydney, Australia
Peter Kang, FDC, Sydney, Australia

OUTSIDE DESIGN CONSULTANTS
Australian Designer
TNB Design, Sydney, Australia
Timothy Bennett, Designer

Lens Chandelier
Limido Comasco, Italy
Adriana Lohmann

SUPPLIERS
Joiners:
Maneto Pty Ltd, Sydney, Australia
Lighting:
LineaLight, Treviso, Italy
GlassiLED Wall:
GlassiLED, Rugby, Great Britain
Traxon Wall:
Osram Australia, Sydney, Australia
Graphics:
BlueStar, Sydney, Australia
Lighting Emitting Panels:
Pixalux, Wollongong, Australia
Props and Equipment:
VDG, Sydney, Australia
Solid Surface:
Staron, Australia, Sydney
Flooring:
Graniti Fiandre S.p.A., Castellarano, Italy

Hudson Grace

San Francisco, CA

SCOPE OF WORK

With a lease signed and the desire to be up and running for the holiday season, the design team was given three months to design the store, fixturing, and millwork, find a general contractor and fixture fabricator, and oversee construction, fabrication, and installation. The client team was focused on developing and articulating the Hudson Grace brand story, finalizing the merchandise direction and securing the opening assortment.

GOALS AND OBJECTIVES

The client wanted to embody simplicity through understated detailing and high quality craftsmanship. The overall result takes its cues from residential design as opposed to a more commercial retail approach.

GOALS ACHIEVED

Success for all efforts depended on a unified and integrated team working closely as decisions were made. This seamless collaboration, where input was welcomed by all core parties, resulted in a

store design, customer experience, and brand story that were immediately embraced within a three month deadline.

BRAND PROMISE

Restraint and design discipline along with modern details, simplicity, and quality reflect the Hudson Grace brand image. The overall store design takes its cues from residential design as opposed to a more commercial retail approach thus referencing the tagline "Hudson Grace . . . A house. A home."

CUSTOMER JOURNEY

The customer journey begins on the sidewalk with an eye catching exterior sign. Inside, customers are free to meander through the freestanding fixtures and along the perimeter shelves to discover the curated product selection that emphasizes the art of home entertaining. Music sets the mood along with the scent of lighted candles. Hudson Grace provides a refreshing shopping experience free of visual, digital, and signage noise.

BRANDING

The store embodies the simplicity required to support the overall marketing message through understated detailing and high quality craftsmanship. Colors are neutral, primarily white and grey with a suggestion of the brand color of International Orange which beckons customers towards the back of the store and outlines the identity signage.

ENVIRONMENTAL GRAPHICS

The storefront exterior reflects the store interior through its dark gray paint with a contrasting taupe entry vestibule. Signage on both the exterior and interior is expressed through stainless steel pin letters outlined in the brand identity color. Product shelf talkers and communication touch points are intentionally limited.

STORE PLANNING

All merchandise is accessible for customers to shop, touch and feel. The display window is a street facing presentation and is also a shop within the shop providing circulation on all sides. The entire store is shop-able and accessible to all customers without barriers.

FIXTURING

Perimeter fixtures perform multiple functions: a display "stage" for product, maximizing merchandise capacity, providing storage for back stock, and conveying the warmth and familiarity of a universal "home" décor. The fixtures feature a modern stairstep crown, chunky adjustable shelves, and storage drawers along the bottom.

FINISHES

Perimeter fixturing provides a warm frame to the merchandise and is juxtaposed against a dark gray background. Loose floor fixtures are fabricated in cold rolled steel tops with dark wood legs. The cash wrap and display pedestals are constructed of ash and stained in a glossy warm white paint finish.

LIGHTING

The white ceiling plane houses a simple grid of track lighting that mirrors the white faux wood plank vinyl flooring. Decorative pendant lights are suspended over display tables and accentuate the simple, modern décor.

VISUAL MERCHANDISING

Given the casual modern residential approach to the design, visual merchandising relies heavily on a stacking and layering product presentation. Stories are told by category—Dinnerware, Serving, Flatware, Barware, Vintage, Home Fragrance, Books, and Linens as well as by material—wood, glass, silver, cashmere, linen, wicker, marble, and ceramics.

DESIGN FIRM
Gensler, San Francisco, CA

PROJECT DESIGN TEAM
Michael Bodziner, Design Director
Debbie Ohlssen, Designer

ARCHITECT
Gensler, San Francisco, CA
Debbie Ohlssen

GENERAL CONTRACTOR
Straub Construction, Fallbrook, CA
Steve Straub

OUTSIDE DESIGN CONSULTANTS

Lighting:
Revolver Design, Berkeley, CA
Michael Webb

Photography:
Matthew Millman

Cannondale Sports Group

233 Glen Cove Road, Carle Place, NY 11514

SCOPE OF WORK

Celebrating a passion for cycling, Cannondale's innovative prototype sets out to redefine the bike retailer model. Extensive research and design efforts went into creating a "hub"; a center of activity that engages, excites, and educates customers, fostering a cycling lifestyle in the community.

GOALS AND OBJECTIVES

With a mission to transform the consumer experience and increase brand awareness, the project team focused on the modern, well-informed, technologically savvy consumer. A distinctive, innovative environment celebrating the brands and community created emotional connections that leads to brand allegiance.

GOALS ACHIEVED

Breaking away from the norm allowed for a truly customer-centric environment. The store engages and excites customers through innovation kiosks, digital technology, a lounge, repair shop, and emphasis on the GURU bicycle fitting system. This prototype can be successfully rolled out in multiple locations to reach a larger customer base.

BRAND PROMISE

This industry-leading innovator fosters the cycling lifestyle in the community with Cannondale brand's "in every household, creating inspired experiences for a fun, healthy world." Customers can rest assured that anything purchased at this store is the best because it was selected by Cannondale for the Cannondale rider.

CUSTOMER JOURNEY

Iconic signage, custom carbon storefront, and "hero" fixture highlighting the latest innovations welcome, educate and connect with customers. Graphic wayfinding along the perimeter and innovation kiosks throughout serve to educate while the customer lounge at the center of the store connects to the community.

BRANDING

Through the use of a neutral palette of grays and metal tones with pops of the brand signature color, a delicate balance between showcasing Cannondale and highlighting the other brands is achieved. Cannondale remains focused on being innovative and sharing the celebration of the cycling lifestyle with its customers.

ENVIRONMENTAL GRAPHICS

Environmental graphics are wayfinding that link categories at the store's perimeter. These combine with graphic signage throughout the store to subtly exemplify the cycling lifestyle. Limited use of brand colors showcases efforts made to balance Cannondale's role as the primary brand, while respecting other featured brands.

STORE PLANNING

Iconic exterior signage and custom carbon storefront combine with a "hero" fixture highlighting the latest brand innovations. A perimeter path links each category while a low, open center drive allows full visibility to the store's rear and centrally located repair shop and welcoming lounge.

FIXTURING

A custom fixture package was designed for this prototype. They consist of clean lines and uncomplicated forms ensuring the products are highlighted and the brand message is consistent. To reflect the brand's core products, high quality, unique materials and full flexibility are integrated into each fixture.

FINISHES

The design pulls from common bike frame materials, specifically carbon fiber, powdercoat paint finishes and rubber. The custom storefront and interior fixtures are adorned with carbon fiber. Mimicking the finish of bike frames and recalling the bike tires and tubes, powdercoat finishes and rubber flooring are applied to fixturing.

LIGHTING

On the sales floor LED lighting was used, including integrated lighting at fixtures, highlighting categories. Consistent color rendition was specified at each fixture ensuring the true colors of all products are displayed, allowing the customer to see the products at their best.

VISUAL MERCHANDISING

Departments are categorized by use and demographic (mountain, road, urban, women's, children's). Paired with creatively displayed products, categories are announced visually with graphics and direct customers to where their interests lie. Each category offers a multi-brand, full assortment of products.

SUSTAINABILITY

LED lighting was installed to enhance the displayed products. Rubber flooring with high post-consumer recycled content was utilized and low VOC paints and low-flow plumbing fixtures were specified. Consumer packaging is made from recycled paper and re-useable bags are available and the mobile POS system allows for paperless transactions.

SALES TECHNOLOGY

To enhance the customer's experience and education related to the cycling lifestyle, iPad adorned kiosks are found on the sales floor and LCD monitors share community events and product information in the customer lounge. Sales associates have handheld checkout capabilities that expedite the checkout process.

DESIGN FIRM
Bergmeyer Associates, Inc.,
Boston, MA

PROJECT DESIGN TEAM
Joseph P. Nevin, Jr., Senior Prinicpal
Stan Kubinski, Senior Project Manager
Sonja Haviland
Stephanie Jones

ARCHITECT
Bergmeyer Associates, Inc.,
Boston, MA
Joseph P. Nevin, Jr., Senior Principal

GENERAL CONTRACTOR
SFV-LLGC, LLC, Redford, MI
Mitch Rosen

OUTSIDE DESIGN CONSULTANTS

Construction Management:
MGAC, New York, NY
Tom Dougherty

Consulting Engineer:
Don Penn Engineering, Grapevine, TX
Hans Oplinger

Structural Engineer:
L.A. Fuess Partners, Boston, MA
Aaron Ford

Permit Expediter:
**Michael F. McNerney Architect,
PLLC,** Nesconset, NY
Mike McNerney

Fixture Contractor:
EMI / All State Fabricators, Tampa, FL
Steve Rooney

Storefront Vendor:
American Products, Inc., Tampa, FL
David LaChapelle

Lighting Vendor:
Capitol Light, Hartford, CT
Jennifer Harrington

Signage Vendor:
Image Works, Inc., Ashland, VA
Michelle Evans

Stockroom Shelving:
Merchandise Equipment Group, Inc.,
Cambridge City, IN
Chris Parker

Burglar Alarm & CCTV:
AFA Protective Systems, Inc.,
Braintree, MA
Joe Cheteoui

AV & Music:
ProMotion Technology Group,
Wixom, MI
Spencer Knisley

Photographer:
Magda Biernat Photography,
Brooklyn, NY
Magda Biernat-Webster

SUPPLIERS

Flooring:

Hard surface (wood, stone, vinyl, etc.):
Mats, Inc., Stoughton, MA (flooring in
sales floor, repair shop, and guru room)
Johnsonite, Chagrin Falls, OH
(flooring in stock room)
Bolon, Stoughton, MA

Flooring:

Soft surface (carpeting):
Interface Flor, LaGrange, GA
(flooring in fitting room)

Ceramic tile (floor & wall):
Daltile, Stoughton, MA (floor and
wall tile in toilet room)

Lighting: (recessed lighting)
Zaneen, Toronto, ON Canada
Phoster, Mount-Royal, QC Canada
3G, Woodbridge, ON Canada
Gotham, Conyers, GA
LC&D, Chatsworth, CA

Track Lighting:
Intense Lighting, Anaheim, CA

Fluorescent:
Lithonia Lighting, Conyers, GA

Pendants/chandeliers:
V2 Lighting, Mountain View, CA
Delray Lighting, Burbank, CA

Fixture Lighting:
Phoster, Mount-Royal, QC Canada
Bartco Lighting, Huntington Beach, CA

Display Lighting:
Winona Lighting, Winona, MN
Acuity Lighting, Conyers, GA (repair
shop)

Fixtures:
Majority provided by **EMI,** Cranston, RI

Project Duo:
Randal Huntington, Design Director,
Springwood, Australia

Custom exterior door handles:
Cannondale Engineers, Bethel, CT

Custom floating resin soffit:
Lightblocks, Nashua, NH

Custom fixture tops:
Lightblocks, Nashua, NH

Countertops:
Silestone, Sugar Land, TX

Slatwall:
Megawall, Comstock Park MI

Metal base/cornerguards:
Diamondlife, Pittsburgh, PA

Laminate:
3M Dynock, St. Paul, MN

Acrylic:
Lightblocks, Nashua, NH

Door Hardware:
**Schlage Ingersoll Rand Security
Technologies Security and Safety
Consultants,** Needham Heights, MA

Furniture:
All Modern Division of Wayfair LLC,
Boston, MA
BoConcepts, Cambridge, MA

Millwork:
EMI, Tampa, FL

Paint finishes:
Benjamin Moore, Montvale, NJ

Plastic Laminates:
Wilsonart, North Reading, MA
Chemetal, Easthampton, MA
Lamin-art, Schaumburg, IL

Fabric finishes:
Mayer Fabric, Indianapolis, IN

Signing/graphics:
Enhance A Colour, Danbury, CT

Pep Boys "Road Ahead" Prototype Store

3933 W Hillsborough Avenue, Tampa, FL 33614

SCOPE OF WORK

Tasking for the designers included providing retail design strategy, re-inventing the interior/exterior store design, developing fixture and adjacency layouts to enhance the customer journey, fixture design/engineering/fabrication/installation, decor design/engineering/installation consulting, interior architecture design intent documentation, furniture specification/procurement and proof of concept project management.

GOALS AND OBJECTIVES

The increase of customer loyalty through an environment elevating the Pep Boys brand, appealing to female customers, creating an inviting customer lounge to grow service business, improving customer flow and encouraging impulse sales through product positioning were among the primary objectives.

GOALS ACHIEVED

All goals were met and many exceeded expectations. The customer lounge was designed to be a comfortable retreat. The store layout was reinvented to create product neighborhoods that were intuitive to navigate. Impulse/accessories were positioned adjacent to the lounge. The parts/service counters were transformed to pods encouraging personalized interaction.

BRAND PROMISE

Pep Boys stands for service and selection. Competitors are either one or the other. To that point, the brand has two distinct types of customers—the do it for me (DIFM) and the do it yourself (DIY). Both customers are equally important and the brand has to stand for "best in class" to each of them, without alienating either.

CUSTOMER JOURNEY

DIFM – The goal was to get them intuitively from the front door to the service consultant, then to the lounge to relax. Products that would appeal to this customer were placed adjacent to the service consultant/lounge, encouraging browsing and add-on sales.
DIY – The object was for the customer to come in and find/get what they needed and leave, while encouraging penetration of the aisles through logical adjacencies, intuitive navigation and strategic exposure to ancillary products.

BRANDING

The design delivers to the brand promise. The tone is friendly and conversational. The customer touch points supporting the service business reflect professionalism and unassuming comfort. The sku-intensive environment showcases an assortment that is second to none. The fixtures, flooring and messaging all support a feeling of added value.

ENVIRONMENTAL GRAPHICS

The brand is all about approachable, helpful and knowledgeable. This Innovation Award: Wayfinding, Signage and Environmental Graphics winner's environment was designed with hyper-intuitive wayfinding through a visually tiered strategy including neighborhood/category/product signage. Customers were empowered to find their own way to the right product without feeling overwhelmed.

STORE PLANNING

The store was divided into neighborhoods situated around a modified racetrack. These neighborhoods facilitated moving customers to areas that could fulfill their "mission" efficiently. The layout encouraged browsing once the "mission" was completed through strategic positioning of categories within the space.

FIXTURING

This project was poised to provide a stellar environment utilizing standard fixtures. One exception was the Featured Item pods to highlight new and innovative product at the front of the store with minimal inventory depth, incorporating feature/benefit information. The result was a modular system that met the goals.

FINISHES

Materials were chosen for durability, ease of maintenance and quality aesthetics. The countertops were stainless steel, the wood-look floors/walls/ceilings/soffits in the lounge and on the column wraps were commercial grade vinyl flooring. A stained concrete floor and logo ensure long lasting durability and low maintenance.

LIGHTING

The interior lighting could not be changed. The exception was the lounge area where recessed lighting was introduced, creating emphasis on walls and the warmth of a coffee shop. The exterior, red lighting strips accentuate the façade-branding beacon, carrying the design language from interior to exterior.

VISUAL MERCHANDISING

Opportunities abound for feature displays and end cap presentations permitting an enhanced assortment of merchandise. New, fashion-forward products made it possible to create a unique, female-targeted accessory area at the front of the store. Expanded racing equipment/accessories resulted in the creation of a "Speed Shop."

DESIGN FIRM
FRCH Design Worldwide,
Cincinnati, OH

PROJECT DESIGN TEAM
Jean-Didier Allonge, VP Creative
Scott Mansfield, Senior Designer
Alexandra Kusick, Designer
Lori Kasten, Sr. Account Director
Janis Healy, VP Retail Strategy

STORE DESIGN TEAM
Tom Carey, Chief Customer Officer
Adam Kondos, Director Creative Services
Craig Keefer, Director Visual Merchandising
Glenn Fink, Director of Development

GENERAL CONTRACTOR
Arrowpoint Facility Services, Weatherford, TX
Jessica Bailey

SUPPLIERS

Exterior Sign Vendor:
Loren Electric Sign Corp., Whittier, CA

Gondola Fixtures:
Lozier Store Fixtures, Omaha, NE

Millwork Fixtures:
EWI Worldwide, Livonia, MI

Decor Graphics:
InnoMark Communications, Fairfield, OH

Flooring:
Centiva, Florence, AL

Patagonia Meatpacking

414 W. 14th Street, New York, NY 10014

SCOPE OF WORK

The project entailed a complete store design in a formerly "white box" space. The store is housed in a renovated landmark building in New York City's historic Meatpacking District.

GOALS ACHIEVED

The store design feels original to the historic building and the neighborhood. With the use of locally sourced reclaimed materials and industrial elements, visitors find it difficult to determine what is new and what is old.

BRAND PROMISE

The brand is an outdoor lifestyle brand. The respect of nature is inherent in Patagonia's DNA and therefore sustainable practice is paramount. Being actively involved within the community is also highly important to the brand.

CUSTOMER JOURNEY

Customers enter a space that appears original with four distinct sales areas: a front room showcasing a genuine meat rail with perimeter display fixtures; a central sales area with cash/wrap; a rear room with lounge; and an auxiliary sales room with rear translucent windows and meat rail display fixtures. Fitting rooms extend around the lounge.

BRANDING

The design emphasizes the brand's commitment to the community by giving back a retail experience in a space that is historically accurate to the neighborhood. The use of locally reclaimed materials and onsite manufacture (reducing embedded energy costs) of architectural elements reinforce the brand's environmental awareness and concerns.

ENVIRONMENTAL GRAPHICS

Exterior signage is produced from oxidized steel to reference the brand's origins as an ironworks company. A sidewall at the front is dedicated as a full bleed photo-wall that provides a backdrop to merchandise that is visible from the storefront.

STORE PLANNING

Several rooms were created to group different merchandise collections. Organized in a linear manner, the store's organization is highly legible. A lounge area with Wi-Fi and access to a drinking fountain help make the store a place of respite.

FIXTURING

A continuous fully functioning meat rail was installed throughout all sales areas. At the front and the auxiliary sales room, the meat rail with the utilization of trolley hooks serves as the primary display fixture. In other areas, the meat rail supports wall fixturing to add depth to the visual display.

PATAGONIA MEATPACKING
Ground Floor

KEY

1. MENSWEAR
2. WOMENSWEAR
3. CASHWRAP
4. LEGACY (HERITAGE) APPAREL
5. LOUNGE
6. FITTING ROOM
7. DRINKING FOUNTAIN
8. BACK OF HOUSE

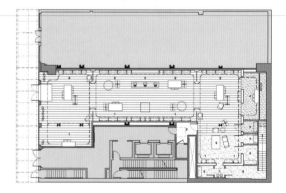

PATAGONIA MEATPACKING
Cellar

KEY

1. BREAK ROOM
2. MANAGER'S OFFICE
3. SHOWER ROOM
4. STOCK
5. BIKE RACKS
6. MEN'S TOILETS
7. WOMEN'S TOILETS

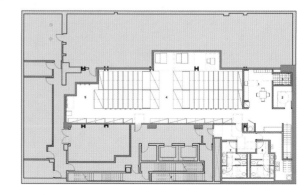

FINISHES

Most of the materials/finishes installed are reclaimed and/or locally sourced: sales area flooring and ceiling beams are reclaimed joists from NYC; brick is reclaimed from Westchester, NY; interior windows, fitting room doors and mirrors were manufactured on site; and fitting room lights and fitting room hooks were made in Brooklyn, NY.

LIGHTING

Feature lights are industrial hazardous fixtures. Fitting room lights are fluorescent, general store lighting in LED.

VISUAL MERCHANDISING

Merchandise is organized by gender with different collections grouped together. Stories are presented on antique furniture and the meat rail is utilized to provide depth. These are further enhanced with anecdotes by brand ambassadors.

SUSTAINABILITY

Locally reclaimed materials were used extensively: sales area flooring and ceiling beams are reclaimed joists from NYC; brick is reclaimed from Westchester, NY. Much was manufactured on site (reducing embedded energy costs): interior windows, fitting room doors and mirrors. Items were locally produced: fitting room lights and fitting room hooks.

SALES TECHNOLOGY

Complementary Wi-Fi is provided to customers throughout the store. The lounge features multimedia sourced from the brand's extensive visual media collection. Customers are able to order merchandise not available in store via the brand's website with the aid of sales associates.

DESIGN FIRM
MNA, New York, NY

PROJECT DESIGN TEAM
Michael Neumann, Principal
Jeff Rudy, Principal
Christine Tan, Senior Designer
Andrew Lee, Designer

STORE DESIGN TEAM
Cathy Weisz
Andy Carlson

ARCHITECT
MNA, New York, NY
Michael Neumann, Principal

GENERAL CONTRACTOR
Tom Hammer Construction LLC,
Raleigh, NC

SUPPLIERS

Thin Brick:
Brick It, Hauppauge, NY

Reclaimed Timber:
The Hudson Company, Brooklyn, NY

Meat Rail:
LeFiell Company, Reno, NV

Sales Feature Lights:
Larson Electronics, Kemp, TX

Fitting Room Light Fixtures:
Fabulux, Inc., Brooklyn, NY

Custom Metal Work:
Free Builders, Bozeman, MT

Wall Fixtures:
Briggs & Sons, Sonoma, CA

Tommy Bahama Bar, Restaurant and Store

551 Fifth Avenue, New York, NY 10017

SCOPE OF WORK

The brand's first flagship store, restaurant and bar located in Manhattan, comprised of 13,000 square feet on two floors in the historic Fred French Building, a landmarked building on Fifth Avenue and 45th Street.

GOALS ACHIEVED

Warm, textural materials that evoke "resort" contrast with raw finishes that lend an urban edge to the palette. Signature elements—such as louvers, screens and lanterns—are sized up to city scale. The restaurant visually expands on the theme while spatially connecting via a double height atrium to the retail area below.

BRAND PROMISE

"Make Life One Long Weekend" is the brand tag line that promises that in an over-scheduled and fast paced world, we can still make room to relax and enjoy life.

CUSTOMER JOURNEY

The customer enters off bustling Fifth Avenue into a calm and airy double height retail space and proceeds deeper into the store to discover a cabana room with linen tenting and a stair up to the second floor restaurant. From the restaurant, the customer can descend a monumental spiral stair into the more intimate Marlin Bar.

BRANDING

The design has direct roots to previous Tommy Bahama stores, but a more sophisticated application of materials and the introduction of edgier elements elevates the brand into its "urban" and urbane incarnation—fulfilling the clients' directive for its first Manhattan flagship.

ENVIRONMENTAL GRAPHICS

Window signage (the Tommy Bahama signature and the Marlin logo) is comprised of backlit channel letters of brass, mounted on the signature louvers, casting a warm and welcoming glow in the windows. The warm materials relate to the material palette of the historic facade.

STORE PLANNING

The customer is immersed in the brand at the first step inside. The loftiness of the space combined with special architectural elements creates an atmosphere that is both relaxed and edgy. The customer is drawn deeper into the space compelled to discover what lies beyond the main space.

FIXTURING

Display fixtures (stacking boxes with brass fittings, leather topped folding tables) are modeled on Napoleonic Campaign furniture that historically was designed to pack-up and move, tying into Tommy Bahama's narrative as an itinerant world traveler. Unique pieces (rope table and 14-foot live edge elm wood table) add delight.

FINISHES

Sandy colored limestone floors, weathered oak plank ceiling and wall, and louvers of reclaimed Coney Island boardwalk are contrasted with the industrial blackened metal display cages and triple height perforated screens with an abstracted palm tree pattern. Millwork of whitewashed poplar and dark stained walnut is detailed with antique brass fittings.

LIGHTING

Oversized, custom lanterns in blackened steel and tarnished brass provide a distinct feature in the atrium. Over-scaled black projector lights are clamped to blackened steel pipes bolted to the oak board ceiling, adding another edgy, industrial touch. Sleek black boxes containing adjustable par lamps are recessed seamlessly in the plank ceiling.

VISUAL MERCHANDISING

Elements of "high" design (brass and crystal chandeliers, antique vitrines) coupled with "low" (whitewashed picnic table and rope ottomans) combine sophistication with relaxation. Tabletop display is designed with blackened iron holding Ipe trays, relating to apparel display systems. Books and found objects support the idea of travel.

SUSTAINABILITY

Reclaimed white oak plank siding on walls and display platforms, and salvaged Coney Island boardwalk repurposed as louvers play a major part in the design. Ceiling fans create an ambiance but also reduce use of air conditioning.

DESIGN FIRM
MNA, New York, NY

PROJECT DESIGN TEAM
MNA:
Visual Merchandising:
Worktable NYC, New York, NY
Deb McKeand

STORE DESIGN TEAM
Frank Kennard
Joseph Stoneburner
Randy Barnsbee
Rob Goldberg
Nick Ragni

ARCHITECT
MNA, New York, NY

GENERAL CONTRACTOR
EW Howell, New York, NY

OUTSIDE DESIGN CONSULTANTS
Engineer (MEP):
Rosini Engineering, PC, New York, NY

Engineer (Structural):
Blue Sky Design, New York, NY

Kitchen:
Post & Grossbard, Inc., Piermont, NY

Lighting:
Schwinghammer Lighting, LLC,
New York, NY

Visual Merchandising / Interior Decoration:
Worktable NYC, Cutchogue, NY

SUPPLIERS
Audio/Visual:
DMX Music, Seattle, WA

Fixtures:
Daniel DeMarco & Associates, Inc.,
Amityville, NY
Amuneal Manufacturing Corp.,
Philadelphia, PA

Kitchen:
Baring Industries, Inc., Parsippany, NY

Lighting: (custom fixtures)
Celadon Group, LLC, New York, NY

Millwork:
Daniel DeMarco & Associates, Inc.,
Amityville, NY
**Jeff Soderbergh, Custom
Sustainable Furnishings,** Newport, RI

Security/CCTV:
Stanley Convergent Security,
Bellevue, WA

Signage/Graphics:
Infinite Manufacturing Group, Inc.,
Irvington, NJ
Color Edge, New York, NY

Stair Fabrication:
Custom Metal Fabricating, Inc.,
Emmaus, PA

Carlo Pazolini Brompton Rd

Brompton Rd., Knightsbridge, London UK

SCOPE OF WORK

Carlo Pazolini flagship store in Knightsbridge, London is a 1700 square foot space housing men's and women's shoes and accessories, located at Brompton Rd in the area of the historical 1900's Brompton Arcade.

GOALS AND OBJECTIVES

As the first store for Carlo Pazolini in the UK, it was vitally important for this location to create brand recognition. Additionally, the design had to entice passersby to enter and become engaged in the displayed product.

GOALS ACHIEVED

The unexpected movement of the unique and highly visible interior in this historical site provided a strong street presence on the highly trafficked Brompton Road. The contrast afforded by the bright, swooping design to the 1900s-era surroundings proved most successful.

BRAND PROMISE

Carlo Pazolini has created its own distinctive, unique and clearly identifiable style, encompassing all the best of Italian tradition, combined with modern design and high-quality materials, making it one of the leaders in the production and sale of shoes in the medium and medium-high price range.

CUSTOMER JOURNEY

The designers created a contemporary barrel vault ceiling as well as the illusion via a mirror wall that the space opens to the exterior at the back. An historical façade detail was used as a generative "seed" for the interior geometric language and led to a pointed rather than semicircular barrel vault design. A tunnel-like twisting of the interior propels the visitor to move through the entire space.

BRANDING

The sleek modern design with the highest-quality Italian crafts-manship, involving minute attention to details and finishes, creates a space that portrays, in the best Italian tradition, the distinctive, unique style Carlo Pazolini desired.

STORE PLANNING

The interior has a tunnel-like twisting wrapping the floor, walls, and ceiling into one another, creates a vortex of movement from front to back in which design elements are moving through a turbulent fluid environment. A mirror wall creates the illusion that the space opens to the exterior at the back, also drawing the visitors into the space.

FIXTURING

Like the buildings we inhabit, we shape our clothing and it shapes us. The designers used the shape of an infant's foot as an iconic "cell" in a network of display shelving and seating. The principle of Swarm Intelligence (i.e.: insect swarms, schools of fish, etc.) was introduced to form loose cellular networks that negotiate an ephemeral distinction between object and space.

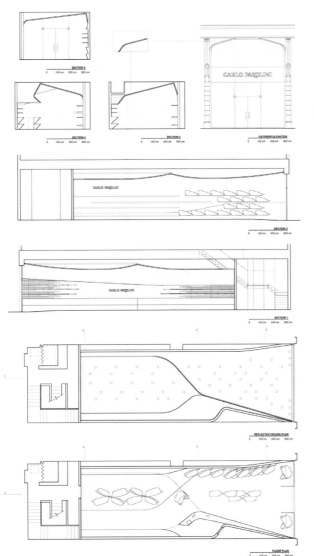

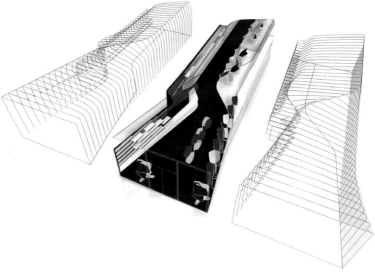

DESIGN FIRM
Giorgio Borruso Design,
Marina Del Rey, CA

PROJECT DESIGN TEAM
Giorgio Borruso Design, Principal
Design

STORE DESIGN TEAM
Simone Domenella

ARCHITECT
Giorgio Borruso Design, Marina Del
Rey, CA
Elizabeth Chang

GENERAL CONTRACTOR
MGPM Ltd., Essex, UK
James Griffith

OUTSIDE DESIGN CONSULTANTS

Lighting:
Studio Luce RemaTarlazzi S.p.A.,
Spain
Stefano Cossiri

SUPPLIERS

Seating and Cell Display Fixtures:
Paola Lenti, Italy

Millwork:
Chiavari, S.r.l., Italy

Lighting:
Targetti, Italy

FINISHES

Enhancing the tunnel twisting effect of the interior, the finishes wrap
around the space. Black tile flooring wraps up the sidewall, until the
wall and shelving change to white a finish. After the peak, it wraps
back over to meet the men's wall in dark slatted wood.

LIGHTING

The lighting in the vaulted ceiling appears random, enhancing the
natural movement of the tunnel-like ceiling. Over the cash and service
area, a soffit is softly backlit with color-changing lighting.

VISUAL MERCHANDISING

The shelving and seating cells in this project use an innovative
molding process which without glue bonds the natural wool and
the resin at a molecular level, forming a new structural composite
that synthesizes old and new, natural and technological further
emphasizing the store's contrast with its surroundings.

Real Madrid Official Store Gran Vía 31

Gran Vía 31, Madrid, Spain

SCOPE OF WORK

Being the official merchandising store for Real Madrid C.F., the design had to be unique and capable of standing out from all other football retail stores. The experience had to be something that a Real Madrid fan wouldn't want to miss, very innovative and cutting-edge, completely focused on the shopping experience and create a lasting impression on the customer.

GOALS ACHIEVED

The main objective was to provide a unique store experience based on Santiago Bernabeu stadium, an experience that reminds us of the effort, dedication and determination needed to achieve glory, a store that teleported the customer to the center of the field, in game action. This was achieved by creating an integrated project that included concept design and commercial implementation, branding, packaging, graphic line and industrial furniture design.

BRAND PROMISE

The brand promise is based on representing the required effort to achieve glory. It is a concept that at the same time honors, praises and immortalizes the club. It states that achievements have been the result of talent, effort, struggle, dedication and determination. The fighting spirit connects the club with its followers, is what makes us great, and what leads us to victory

CUSTOMER JOURNEY

The customer enters the store submerging himself in a crowded stadium. The exhibition areas are clearly divided, the cash-wrap stands out, legendary players on the walls and furniture recall the club's majestic sports career. A goal is scored, the stadium roars, the public take pictures and the customer feels as if he were in the middle of the game

BRANDING

The store walls recreate the Santiago Bernabeu Stadium; the players reflected on these walls are legends that have been indispensable for the greatness and immortality of the club. The stadium's central marquee is reinterpreted to highlight the store cash-wrap, accompanied by a media wall lined with victories that illustrate the club's glory.

ENVIRONMENTAL GRAPHICS

Consists of walls that teleport the customer to the center of the field: the sensation of a crowded stadium, taking pictures, cheering, legendary players honoring the club's history, today's players captured on the furniture, a panel lined with victories. It's the combination of all these elements that emphasizes the brand message.

STORE PLANNING

The store is divided into three exhibition areas: Textile Zone (official gear and training), Merchandising Zone and Adidas Zone. In the basement of the store we find a Special Corner, a thematic space that changes over time capable of presenting unique thematic products, currently this space is themed as a Real Madrid bathroom.

FIXTURING

All furniture is modular and was designed with the concept "Ready to Assemble Modular Design," designing the smallest piece for its intelligent assembly system. This allows maximum flexibility, versatility of distribution, standardization in quality and more sustainable transportation by optimizing the dimensions and logistics for international expansion.

FINISHES

The materials chosen were based on selecting the most appropriate materials following strict criteria to balance between esthetics and durability, having to respond to a modern and futuristic design. Gypsum board was chosen for the ceiling designs and lacquered wood for the furniture. The entire store has vinyl flooring and all façade windows are made of insulated glass.

LIGHTING

The entire store is equipped with LED illumination: general, key and decorative. The later integrates LEDs into the images on the walls to create the effect of the public taking flash pictures. These LEDs are synchronized with the in-store multimedia system and are activated when a goal occurs on the media wall screens while listening to the sounds of a crowded stadium.

VISUAL MERCHANDISING

All visual merchandising was designed and integrated into the store based on a POP (point of purchase) advertising system, including the commercial slogan "Glory is Not by Chance" and several phrases that accompany the slogan. All furniture has color stripes for easy product identification, product type labels and graphic content to emphasize the product and persuade the customer.

SUSTAINABILITY

100% of the store is equipped with next-generation LED luminaries with maximum energy efficiency. The HVAC systems are optimized for maximum performance to minimize energy consumption. The store entrance is designed with a double HVAC sealing system. An automated gate that opens only when the customer enters or leaves and has an air curtain that works intelligently.

SALES TECHNOLOGY

Besides having tablets to interact with web media, in-store aromas, and shirt customization, the store is equipped with an "intelligent WiFi counter" that communicates with the customer's phone. This system retrieves useful information such as how many people entered, floor visited, time spent inside, and where they are from, invaluable information to understand the customer's needs and manage the store.

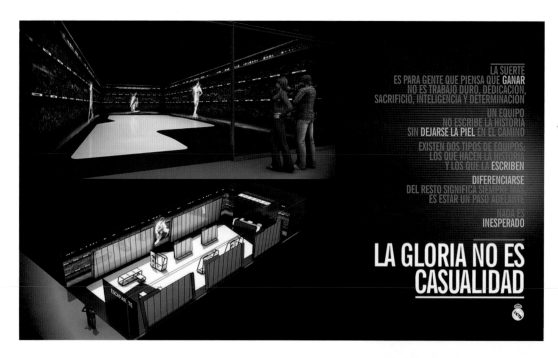

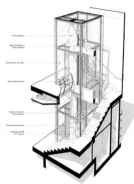

DESIGN FIRM
sanzpont (arquitectura),
Barcelona, Spain

PROJECT & STORE DESIGN TEAM
Sergio Sanz Pont
Victor Sanz Pont
Miguel Angel Mendez Andrade
Jose-Miguel Cano Mendez
Jose Garcia Madrid
Mariano Aguado de Sas
Leobardo Martinez
Oscar Sanz Pont
Gerard Delgado Bargallu
David Guitierrez Gungora
Tania Cota Ocho

ARCHITECT
sanzpont (arquitectura), Barcelona,
Spain
Sergio Sanz Pont, Barcelona, Spain
Victor Sanz Pont, Cancun, Mexico

GENERAL CONTRACTOR
**CYC Construcciones (Boadilla del
Monte)**

OUTSIDE DESIGN CONSULTANTS
Technical & Financial Consultants:
CREA Projects / Areas S.A.,
Barcelona, Spain

SUPPLIERS
Furniture Fabrication:
Martinez Otero, Pontevedra, Spain

Graphic Design, Store Packaging:
LDG, Barcelona, Spain

Retail Business Development:
Areas S.A. / Adidas

Project Management:
Areas S.A.

Structure & MEP:
Ibinser S.L.

Lighting:
Performance in Lighting / Lledu

Multimedia, Audio & Smell:
**Trison Ac˙stica / BBgreen /
akewuele**

Visual Components:
aura / print it!

READY TO ASSEMBLE MODULAR DESIGN

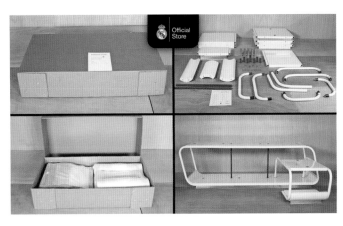

Patagonia Bowery

313 Bowery, New York, NY 10003

SCOPE OF WORK

The designers were tasked a complete gut renovation of an existing retail space, new storefront, and new MEP. Most of the structurally compromised floor required reinforcement and replacement.

GOALS AND OBJECTIVES

The sole objective was to create the first east coast Patagonia surf shop by layering materials and history in the former CB's 313 Gallery, an extension of CBGB.

GOALS ACHIEVED

The store design feels original to the historic building and to the neighborhood.

BRAND PROMISE

The brand is an outdoor lifestyle brand with this particular location focusing on surf. The store has a relaxed and laid back atmosphere.

CUSTOMER JOURNEY

Customers enter through a surf montage, encounter a surf board display area showcasing and explaining the different boards on offer, a central lounge and casual cash/wrap area, fitting rooms, and accessories towards the back. There is an event space on the lower level.

BRANDING

A brand focusing on the fundamentally laid back surfing lifestyle is brought to this historic building and neighborhood and is reflected in the store's relaxed atmosphere.

PATAGONIA BOWERY

Ground Floor

KEY

1. MENSWEAR
2. SURFBOARDS
3. SURFBOARD DISPLAY
4. LOUNGE
5. CASHWRAP
6. FITTING ROOMS
7. ACCESSORIES
8. WETSUITS
9. WOMENSWEAR
10. BACK OF HOUSE

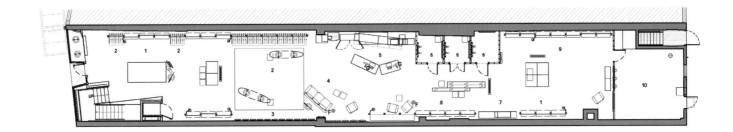

ENVIRONMENTAL GRAPHICS

Signage, including storefront and interior signage is of oxidized metal. The store is linear in nature and is easily legible.

STORE PLANNING

At the entrance customers are introduced to the surfing lifestyle via a surf montage. Their path leads to a surfboard display area, a central lounge and cash/wrap area. Fitting rooms and accessories are located toward the rear of the store. On the lower level there is an event space.

FIXTURING

Retired NYC sidewalk scaffolding was repurposed as posts for the perimeter system. Hardware for merchandising was custom designed and built. New and used furniture, cabinets, and desks were sourced individually and collaged together to create the cash/wrap and back/wrap as well as sales fixtures

FINISHES

Reclaimed Heart Pine Flooring from a former factory in Bayonne, NJ, was staggered in to replace damaged floorboards.

LIGHTING

Sales areas feature Barn Light Electric pendant lights. The sales area spot lighting is all LED. Fitting room light fixtures were custom designed and manufactured.

VISUAL MERCHANDISING

Surfboards for sale provide appropriate visual merchandising. These are displayed front on, sideways and on surfboard stands. Additional elements include, wetsuits, and paddles. Books, memorabilia and sports trophies are displayed in areas to reinforce the casual surf vibe.

SUSTAINABILITY

Existing material was used where possible. Newly installed wood floors, wood beams, fitting room doors and door hardware are reclaimed, as are the scaffolding wall fixtures. Additionally, most of the store furniture is reclaimed.

DESIGN FIRM
MNA, New York, NY

PROJECT DESIGN TEAM
Michael Neumann, Principal
Jeff Rudy, Principal
Christine Tan, Senior Designer
Andrew Lee, Designer

STORE DESIGN TEAM
Cathy Weisz
Andy Carlson

ARCHITECT
MNA, New York, NY
Michael Neumann, Principal

GENERAL CONTRACTOR
Tom Hammer Construction LLC,
Raleigh, NC

SUPPLIERS

Reclaimed Flooring and Baseboard:
The Hudson Company, Brooklyn, NY

Fitting Room Light Fixtures:
Fabulux, Inc., Brooklyn, NY

Reclaimed Doors and Door Hardware:
Olde Good Things, New York, NY

Sofa:
Fridgecouch, New Bedford, MA

Under Armour Brand House

700 S President St., Baltimore, MD 21202

SCOPE OF WORK

Under Armour and a+I developed the initial concept and design while Chandler Inc. served as design engineer of this engaging retail environment that brings to life the passion and determination that drives athletes of all types and abilities. The focus was on innovation and design as a tool to guide customers and make recommendations that would be specific to their needs and objectives.

GOALS AND OBJECTIVES

Using good design and innovation Under Armour sought to provide consumers with an elevated shopping experience through the use of technology, imagery and education. They wanted to offer the largest depth of merchandise possible that catered to all types of athletes; including women, children, professionals and amateurs. The creation of the store was also meant to display their support in the development and enhancement of the local Baltimore community.

GOALS ACHIEVED

The state-of-the-art interactive Innovation Center showcases Under Armour's most current technology driven performance gear. Digital displays, large scale lifestyle graphics and trained product category experts inform, inspire and engage consumers on all different levels of the shopping experience. The store features an expanded merchandise selection for women and children. Large lifestyle graphics and iconic Baltimore imagery of athletes and icons reinforce Under Armour's commitment to enhancing Baltimore's image and continuing to drive home a sense of community.

BRAND PROMISE

The essence of the Under Armour brand is performance driven apparel that empowers athletes of all types to commit and improve. The brand statement, "I Will" is meant to evoke passion and drive

energy to achieve and succeed.

CUSTOMER JOURNEY

The customer journey is intended to convey the brand image, educate and provide a dynamic retail experience. Technology integration throughout of the store reinforces the Under Armour brand and provides different layers of information. The large 3D logo serves as the backdrop for the cash wrap. Merchandise is showcased to create a broad and bright color palate and the custom footwear area is designed for shopper comfort. Finally, customers navigate to the Corian clad cash-wrap with inlaid touchscreen monitors.

BRANDING

The high performance nature of the brand and desire for broader demographic appeal are conveyed through the open, inviting and colorful store. The merchandise in displayed in a unique manner (example floating shoe wall) and the gear is brought to life through live and static imagery.

ENVIRONMENTAL GRAPHICS

Large-scale images of athletes competing or performing are incorporated into floor fixtures, wall bays and fitting rooms. The large jumbo-tron and other screens display images of local teams and events, and Under Armour merchandise in performance mode.

STORE PLANNING

The store layout is designed to tell a story and guide the consumer through all aspects of the Under Armour brand. The shoe area is customized with comfortable throne seating, the fitting rooms feature lounge seating and inspirational images. The journey ends with a large custom 3D logo that flanks the Corian clad cash wrap.

FIXTURING

Fixturing includes tables, platforms, mannequins and kiosks to accommodate merchandise of all types and sizes. The wall bays feature the universal Garcy's Stud System to showcase merchandise at different levels and be easily interchangeable. All featured merchandise is accessible to allow consumers to touch/feel all product.

FINISHES

The use of architectural materials (metal, cement, Corian, Straight Grain Douglas Fir) creates an environment that conveys high performance, strength and determination in a unique manner.

LIGHTING

Lighting is incorporated into many elements of the store design. Wall bays feature custom inlaid LED lighting to highlight products. Overhead lights are set to keep the store bright and open while additional backlit features (on the cash/wrap, logo wall and in the fitting rooms) create a softer look and provide a beacon effect for shoppers.

VISUAL MERCHANDISING

From a visual standpoint the store's color palate is set around the merchandise currently on display. The look and feel of the store changes depending upon the season and what merchandise is priority. The movable graphic elements in the backwall and features on the large jumbo-screen add another layer to the store, reinforce the brand and drive home the performance driven concept.

Chandler, Inc., Afton, MN.

PROJECT DESIGN TEAM
Under Armour, Baltimore, MD
Tom Walsh, Senior Director of Retail
Store Development
Patrick Stringer, Project Manager,
Retail Store Development
Nora Kenney, Retail Store
Development Manager

ARCHITECT DESIGN FIRM
**architecture + information, New
York**
Bradley Zizmor
Dag Folger
Phil Ward
Will Rosebro
Aaron Whitney
Chris Evans

**DESIGN ENGINEERING &
FABRICATION**
Chandler, Inc. Minnesota

GENERAL CONTRACTOR
MacKenzie Contracting, Baltimore,
MD

SUPPLIERS

Audio/Visual:
Activate the Space, Canton, CT

Stretched Ceiling System:
Newmat USA, West Babylon, NY

Custom Fixtures:
Chandler, Inc. Afton, MN

Flooring/Carpet:
Bentley Prince Street, Los Angeles,
CA

Flooring/Wood:
Robbins Sports Surfaces,
Cincinnati, OH

Furniture Upholstery:
SIXINCH, Goshen, IN

Lighting:
Wiedenbach Brown, New York, NY

Lighting Consultant:
Lighting Workshop, New York, NY

Mannequins:
Forms-Goldsmith, New York, NY

CA Exterior Signage:
Adart Sign Company,
San Francisco, CA

Custom Wall Coverings:
Duggal Visual Solutions, New York, NY

Exterior Custom Gate:
Schweiss Doors, Fairfax, MN

Concrete Contractor:
Ohio Cemtech, Cincinnati, OH

In-wall Standards/Bracket System:
Triad Manufacturing, St. Louis, MO

Custom Shoe Displays
Cubic Visual Systems, Burnsville, MN

Metal Components:
Reeve Store Equipment Company,
Pico Rivera, CA

*made fresh!

CARDS ✳ GIFTS
GREATER
GOODS
GIVING BACK

CHANDLER

Charming Charlie - Store of the Future

420 Meyerland Plaza, Houston, TX 77096

SCOPE OF WORK

The design team was asked to create a new design concept for the store including space planning, storefront design, graphic application, furniture selection, fixture design, finishes, merchandising and lighting.

GOALS AND OBJECTIVES

Charming Charlie wanted to create a new store prototype that would appeal to a broad demographic of customers and feature as many as 40,000 units of merchandise. The client also wanted to reduce the size of the store from 7,500 square feet to 4,000 square feet.

GOALS ACHIEVED

The store design refreshes the brand and appeals to women of all ages. Products are intentionally organized to appeal to customers who enjoy "the hunt" and celebrate "the find." Fixtures were designed to be flexible with easily interchangeable modules that can be changed to display a variety of merchandise.

BRAND PROMISE

The brand promise is "fun," "colorful" and "affordable" fashion accessories organized by color and trend. CC wants to help every woman "find her fabulous." It celebrates color, style and making a statement.

CUSTOMER JOURNEY

Bold store graphics, rotating storefront displays and slanted walls entice customers into the store. Merchandise is organized by color and trend. The store is divided into style zones organized around a central style bar. "Charmers" assist shoppers in putting their look together aided by iPads and video.

BRANDING

The new store delivers on fun and style in a big way. It's polished, enticing, bright and colorful. It's easy to navigate and simple to finalize purchases. Branding is incorporated throughout as is key messaging.

ENVIRONMENTAL GRAPHICS

The CC logo is incorporated into the store design as a decorative element. End caps of the fixtures feature full-height style messaging. Video monitors throughout the store illustrate style trends and incorporate key messaging.

STORE PLANNING

The team brought an online shopping experience into the brick and mortar store. Merchandise is edited and arranged in an ROYGBIV pinwheel surrounding a central Style Bar. The in-store experience transports shoppers into the pages of the latest fashion magazine through the use of graphics, video and personal attention.

FIXTURING

Charming Charlie fixtures and displays were scaled to provide easy access and ergonomic support for shoppers of all shapes and sizes. Fixtures also store back merchandise for ease of restocking. Despite the large amount of merchandise in the store, shoppers can easily navigate and find what they need.

FINISHES

Furniture and fixtures were locally sourced and manufactured. Fixtures were designed in a white lacquered finish to create a clean, contemporary backdrop for the product. Dark flooring creates a dramatic counterpoint to the fixtures and makes the merchandise "pop."

LIGHTING

Crystal chandeliers are a recognizable feature of Charming Charlie stores. These classic fixtures were mixed with a selection of contemporary pendant lights and glowing display surfaces to provide flattering light levels that showcase the merchandise and the customer.

VISUAL MERCHANDISING

Each style section features fixtures with multiple layers and interchangeable modules inspired by traditional ladies' dressing tables. Customers are encouraged to bring their selections to the style bar and use style trays inspired by jewelry boxes to create their individualized "look" with the help of a stylist "Charmer."

SUSTAINABILITY

Materials, fixtures and furniture were locally sourced. Natural light is provided throughout the store.

DESIGN FIRM
Gensler, Houston, TX

PROJECT DESIGN TEAM
Lisa Pope-Westerman, Design Director
Sean Thackston, Senior
Laura Hastik, Designer
Caroline Lemoine, Designer
June Estrella, Job Captain
Steffany Orjuela, Graphic Design

ARCHITECT
Gensler, Houston, TX
Ann Kifer

SUPPLIERS
IDX (fixtures), Earth City, MO
Special Lighting Group, Centerbrook, CT
Pantheon Tile, Carrolton, TX

Fresh St. Market

1650 Marine Drive, West Vancouver, BC V7V 1J1 Canada

SCOPE OF WORK

The project was to convert a Safeway store into a completely new grocery destination in the affluent neighborhood of West Vancouver, BC. Services provided included full creative concept starting with brand identity and application, branding and logo, positioning in marketplace, interior/exterior design and planning, signage, graphics, finishes, lighting, and installation supervision.

GOALS AND OBJECTIVES

H.Y. Louie, a leading Canadian food retailer, recognized grocery market saturation with "middle of the road" retailers. The grocer was seeking to make an impact by giving its customers an unprecedented grocery experience with a real (versus smoke and mirrors) focus on fresh with its new brand concept. The client goals were to highlight the market position of "affordable fresh."

GOALS ACHIEVED

The emphasis was on locality: aesthetic, producers, foods, programs. The achieved vision was to load one side (one half) of the store, with fresh fare—a collection of boutiques-within-store, each a purveyor of fresh foods (cheese, bakery, butcher, deli)—rather than around the perimeter. Produce is visibly exciting, front and center, upon entering the space. In interpreting the Fresh St. Market service vision into a physical storefront, lighting and display were key to emphasizing the freshness, quality, and colorful aspects of each category of food.

BRAND PROMISE

Fresh St. Market is a place to explore, discover, and try what's fresh, great, amazing and delicious. They search far and wide for the tastiest, freshest affordable foods. The store exemplifies a feeling of fun, wonder, and most importantly, a playground of fresh ingredients to combat the middle of the road grocery feeling of their competitors.

CUSTOMER JOURNEY

The customer journey is designed to mirror a visit to an urban fresh market, such as one finds on the streets of Paris, with food stalls flowing together and into brick-and-mortar shops. Destination areas are employed as visual focal points. Each department acts as a boutique within-store giving an authentic, seafront farmers market flavor. The design parallels the brand's core standards: freshness, locality, aesthetic, and good taste.

BRANDING

There's integrity in the way the design delivers the brand promise of exploration, discovery, and ultimately an experience in freshness. This means an authentic "street or waterfront market" presentation, and loading over half the space with in-store boutique destinations focuses on fresh fare.

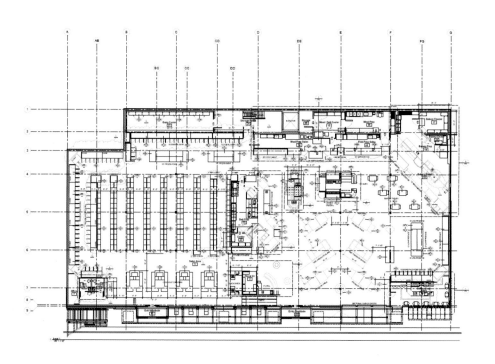

ENVIRONMENTAL GRAPHICS

Dimensional copy highlights specific departments (e.g., 13 Bakers, Chop House). Various hanging banner signs, framed chalkboards, corkboards and even brown parchment paper on roll were incorporated as promotional messaging.

STORE PLANNING

The store's layout mirrors its urban fresh feel with destination areas employed as visual focal points. Each department acts as a boutique-within-store giving an authentic, seafront farmers market.

FIXTURING

The designers were given liberty to provide various custom fixtures with a focus on creating bright, unique ways to display fresh food. A great example is the Soup & Salad Bar Island. The vertical materials included corrugated steel and wood grain around the island, topped with a Caesarstone countertop.

FINISHES

The color concept of surgical white, crisp black, rustic textured materials, and the boldest colors found in "nature's kitchen" references the urban foodie who inspires the space. Simple, rustic materials were used throughout – this included exposed grain edges of wood and metallic features.

LIGHTING

A lighting design concept was incorporated that offered plenty of dramatic, ambient illumination and product placement lighting to provide the perfect amount of twinkle to showcase the plethora of fresh ingredients in the store.

VISUAL MERCHANDISING

Thoughtful, visual displays dedicated to each "food destination" are a major part of this design. In keeping with the street market persona, displays incorporate rustic materials, merchandise is piled organically, literally overflowing with freshness, as one would find in a fish market, corner bakery, or indie food stall.

DESIGN FIRM
King Retail Solutions,
Eugene, OR

PROJECT & STORE DESIGN TEAM
Christopher Studach
Marco Ingracio
Anna Victoria
Tim McCall

ARCHITECT
Chandler Associates Architecture
Inc., Vancouver, BC Canada
Curtis Brock

GENERAL CONTRACTOR
Norson Construction Ltd.,
Vancouver, BC Canada
Scott Lussier

SUPPLIERS
Century Signs & Awnings,
Vancouver, BC Canada
Brencar, Inc., Vancouver, BC Canada
Jones Food Store Equipment Ltd.,
Vancouver, BC Canada

There are design firms and there are build vendors. And there's us. We just plain work better.

With early roots as a production shop, we design and build retail environments with every aspect in mind. What do you want the shopper to feel? Where do you want them to move? How much will it cost to install and maintain? How will it wear? Can it even be built economically?

When you approach a design challenge holistically, rather than piece-meal, the end result just plain works better.

KING RETAIL SOLUTIONS

KRS

Fresh St. Farms, British Columbia

No Frills Stratford

618 Huron Street, Stratford, ON Canada

SCOPE OF WORK

The scope was to modernize Canada's favorite discount grocer. This included the redesign of the trading identity, interiors and all graphics including uniforms and packaging.

GOALS AND OBJECTIVES

The goal was to refresh the business, retaining the existing customer base whilst also attracting a wider more savvy audience. To do this the designers needed to more clearly represent the No Frills core value proposition by better expressing their expertise in a fresh and modern environment.

GOALS ACHIEVED

The modernization has been spectacularly successful, exceeding the client's sales expectations to such a degree that a national rollout of the new décor and branding concept will be accelerated.

BRAND PROMISE

"Simple, honest, local value-for money-grocer" is the image that No Frills wishes to maintain. This makeover has realized this goal most successfully.

CUSTOMER JOURNEY

The designers better defined the fresh hall by introducing a "palette" wall and warmer lighting. Signage helps the customer at multiple points throughout the store and "specials" are integrated departmentally. Yellow and timber wall finishes make the journey more enjoyable. Results have delivered increased customer visits and increased revenues.

BRANDING

Every aspect of the trading identity was reviewed to strike the correct balance between value and experience and to embody the brand's promise of "A Smart Place to Shop." The new No Frills store offers customers a friendly local supermarket that is passionate about quality and value.

ENVIRONMENTAL GRAPHICS

The overall design and cost of the fit-out was determined by the low cost, franchised supermarket situated in a standalone suburban building. Store planning and circulation within a singular rectangular building allowed focus on planning the customer's journey starting with colorful produce and ending with frozen food.

STORE PLANNING

Store planning was approached with strong ideas to represent the brand. The low cost franchised supermarket in a standalone suburban building drove the overall design and cost of the fit-out. Store planning and circulation within a singular rectangular building allowed the designers to concentrate on the journey approach through colorful fresh produce, deli, bakery, meats, dairy, and grocery products simplifying the journey through the store

FIXTURING

The fixtures in the store reflect the brand—unfussy, uncluttered and simple. Materials include a ground and polished concrete floor, simple supermarket fixtures with low-cost finishes with strong brand colors introduced for warmth. A grid ceiling above fresh produce allows lighting attachments and adds strong color to the product.

FINISHES

A palette was selected to suit the brand and emphasize store and product valuet—polished pebble concrete floor, large grain particle-board bulkheads and a wall of timber skids dividing the fresh food hall from the grocery. Signage and wayfinding complement the brand in yellow and red. The ceiling is an open truss system with a visible metal deck roof. The staff wears specially designed t-shirts emblazoned with "still bananas."

DESIGN FIRM

Brand strategy, Interior Design, Branding, In-store Graphics, Packaging and Uniform Design
Landini Associates
Sydney, NSW, Australia

ARCHITECT

Turner Fleischer Architects
Toronto, ON Canada

GENERAL CONTRACTOR
StuCor Construction Ltd., Jordan Station, ON Canada
Brian Gill

SUPPLIERS

Structural Engineer:
CPE Structural Consultants Ltd., Toronto, ON Canada

Mechanical Engineer:
LKM, Division of SNC-Lavalin Inc., Toronto, ON Canada

Electrical Engineer:
Hammerschlag & Joffe Inc., Toronto, ON Canada

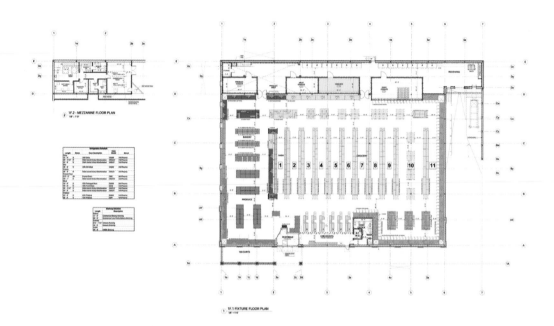

Founded in 1993, Landini Associates is a multi-disciplinary retail design and brand consultancy consisting of strategic planners, architects and interior, graphic and product designers. We produce world class, simple yet effective work that lasts. We are interested in the classic over the fashionable and many of our projects have a longevity that exceeds the market norm.

Strategically driven but creatively led, we are equally at ease inventing new brands as we are evolving and redefining existing ones. We bring about a fusion of multiple disciplines resulting in an end product with a singular vision. This results in the best possible outcome for both our clients and their customers.

Landini Associates is based in Sydney and is currently working in North America and Canada, the UAE, the UK, Asia and Australia. Clients include Loblaws, T2 (Unilever), Jones the Grocer (LVMH), Amore Pacific (Primera, Mamonde, Innisfree, Lirikos), Hilton Hotels, Westpac Bank Australia, Jurlique, Coles, Woolworths, and various independents.

—
studio@landiniassociates.com
landiniassociates.com

Landini Associates
Design and Brand Consultants

DFS Wine & Cigars

DFS Galleria, Four Seasons Hotel Macau, The Cotai Strip, Cotai, Macau

SCOPE OF WORK

The designers were tasked to plan, design and document a wine and cigar specialty shop elevated to DFS luxury positioning while conveying merchandise expertise and innovation in a traditional category.

GOALS & OBJECTIVES

Through the introduction and use of simple architecture, detail and materials, the goal for the designers was to communicate merchandise dominance and creatively showcase product via innovative presentation.

GOALS ACHIEVED

With successful retail planning, high-end brand presentation, simple yet sophisticated materials, and clean, clear and elegant visual merchandising, the store warmly invites shoppers to an oasis of decadent delight.

BRAND PROMISE

Building on the ultimate luxury positioning of DFS Galleria's Wine and Cigars is a category specialty store that delivers a superior merchandise assortment of old and new world wines and cigars. Through extraordinary services such as wine tasting, special promotional events, cigar humidor and true customer service expertise, shoppers experience the ultimate in product and service.

CUSTOMER JOURNEY

Holidaymakers can easily orientate themselves for self-selection through the mid floor and side perimeters while the rear features a large walk-in climate controlled room reserved for a superior vintage assortment. A refined signage system communicates origin of the wine and cigar merchandise. Customer service expertise is never far away with sales associates trained to expose customers to new offers point of purchase displays, table top promotions and a wine tasting area.

BRANDING

Branding is built upon the ultimate luxury positioning of DFS Galleria's, Wine & Cigars that delivers a superior merchandise assortment of old and new world wines and cigars.

ENVIRONMENTAL GRAPHICS

Category, origin, vintage and price graphic communication eases customer orientation and facilitates self-selection across all offers. Perimeter lifestyle graphics communicate wine growing heritage in a sepia tone sun-lit vineyards via internally illuminated light boxes. LCD screens integrated into selected wall presentations add an important layer of depth of motion and information.

STORE PLANNING

An open shop front exposes the entire range and simple plan of the space. Easy to shop and self-select mid-floor fixture systems facilitate flow through the shop and to perimeter walls. Featured are climate control rooms of vintage wine and a cigar humidor. Customer service and cash wrap is located logically at the transition between wine and cigar climate controlled rooms.

FIXTURING

Mid-floor feature tables remain flexible for a variety of stack up presentations and can be cleared for the hosted wine events. The vertical nature of the perimeter design lends itself well to the merchandise presentation. Special vertical "shards" dangle from the ceiling holding a single bottle each within an internally illuminated glow.

FINISHES

Narrow grain wood in a medium tone complements the linear forms of the perimeter architecture. Lighter tone wood frames the perimeter of the shop and light marble on the flooring and table-tops. Limestone panels are used on the façade and the wine room.

LIGHTING

The overall lighting concept utilizes recessed LED spotlights with a focused attention and light level that creates depth and contrast to maximize the significant ceiling height. Decorative pendant "shard" light fixtures provide additional interest and accent mid-floor. Rear lit vertical fins in a very warm color create further interest and depth.

VISUAL MERCHANDISING

Tabletop presentation allows the potential for a variety of abundant presentations using wine crates and props to present featured wines. Vintage highlight bays within the climate controlled wine room tell the story of the wine maker and vineyard and present the prestigious merchandise on angled wooden wave profile shelves. Perimeter fixtures and merchandise presentation are constructed from vertical bands of narrow grain wood punctuated with shadow boxes for magnum and accessories presentation and are rear illuminated for affect.

DESIGN FIRM
rkd retail/iQ, Bangkok, Thailand

PROJECT DESIGN TEAM

RKurt Durrant, Principal in Charge
Warisa Laingchaikul, Creative Director
Thapanee Chirathitapa, Interior Designer
Valan Panichnok, Senior Graphic Designer
Mit Seehamat, Senior DDI
Thawatchai Tiemjarat, Head CG/3D

STORE DESIGN TEAM

Tim DeLessio, President Group East
Linda Krueger, VP, Worldwide Store Development
Kevin Tranbarger, VP, Business Development
Andrew Gibb, Director, Store Development
Graeme Fowler, VP, Global Visual Merchandising

OUTSIDE DESIGN CONSULTANTS

Lighting:
Iguzzini, Hong Kong
Richard Leung

Zumbo Melbourne

12-14 Claremont Street, South Yarra, VIC 3141 Australia

SCOPE OF WORK

The designers were tasked with the installation of creative fit-out on the walls, furniture design and manufacture, graphic vinyl application on the windows, graphic development of neon signage and branding.

GOALS & OBJECTIVES

The designers envisaged an engaging interior treatment reflecting and celebrating the intense and colorful dessert and pastry products on display. Concepts were explored including Victorian-era architectural ornamentation. From architecture to graphic design, this is a multidisciplinary effort showcasing Zumbo as no ordinary patissier.

GOALS ACHIEVED

A lot of trial and error and creative and practical experimentation were expended to successfully master the required materials and techniques within a strict budget. The time constraints forced most work to be completed after hours but nonetheless the design was not compromised. The designers achieved what they originally set out to do and the client was ecstatic with the result.

BRAND PROMISE

The Zumbo brand attributes of experimental, energetic, playful and bizarre are evident in the furniture, wall panels and the custom graphic identity including the neon sign and window artwork. Eccentric furniture and exotic vinyl window graphics help frame and brand the action going on within the store.

CUSTOMER JOURNEY

Outside the store the customer is greeted by the intense pink glow from the neon sign. Then, as you enter, ice cream cake furniture pieces and a surreal display of mirrors emphasize the vibrant desserts arranged in large cabinets. This spectacle is framed by the graphic application on the store's large windows.

BRANDING

The neon logo designed for the Melbourne store embodies all the eccentricities of the already established brand but is done in a way that serves as a signature for the Melbourne, and more specifically the South Yarra area, installation.

ENVIRONMENTAL GRAPHICS

The color pink is largely featured throughout the installation. In an effort to divert the overall design from potentially being too sweet and innocent, the window graphics are deliberately black and slightly grotesque. The pink also serves to neatly frame the vivid display happening inside from the front window through to the side alley.

STORE PLANNING

The store is centered around a large display cabinet (selected by the client) which formed the basis of the circulation plan. Working off the linear nature of this piece, the planning of the space aimed to create a separate customer zone, allowing customers to peruse the products while also being engaged by the space.

FIXTURING

The design on the sidewall allows for functional joinery and cabinetry to be below waist level while permitting a floating black shelf to hold the merchandise and packaging for display. This serves as a backdrop for the customer who sees these products at eye level as they are being served.

FINISHES

One of the primary aims of the design was to accentuate the colorful nature of the product, so formed mirror polycarbonate and polished stainless steel were the predominant finishes used. This allowed for a highly reflective surface that mirrored and refracted the products and merchandise.

LIGHTING

A pink neon light sits on the back wall, creating an ambient glow throughout the entire retail space. Working with the reflective nature of the interior surfaces, it draws attention into the store from the street. The neon light is supplemented by a single track suspended below the ceiling line with angled spotlights.

VISUAL MERCHANDISING

The design of the space aims to emphasize the products and merchandise by reflecting and thus enlarging the presentation of the product. The furniture creates a visual link to the products and branding appearing as an enlarged version of one of the cakes that might be sold. The staff zones behind the counter are black by comparison to visually recede into the space.

DESIGN FIRM
Elenberg Fraser, Melbourne, VIC Australia

PROJECT & STORE DESIGN TEAM
Callum Fraser, Director
Thomas Orton, Architect
Kim Lai, Architect
Reade Dixon, Associate
Richard Pattison, Interior Designer
Elizabeth White, Interior Designer
Jansen Aui, Graduate Architect
Peter Scott, Graduate Architect
Emily Polidano, Graphic Designer
Toby Flaye, Graduate Architect
Michael Murdock, Graduate Architect

Jaime Sol, Graduate Architect
Sonali Peris, Interior Designer
Elizabeth Westworth, Graduate Architect
Yunwei Xu, Graduate Architect
Stella Lien, Graduate Architect
Alex Hopkins, Interior Designer

ARCHITECT
Elenberg Fraser, Melbourne, VIC Australia

JaBistro

222 Richmond Street West, Toronto, ON M5V 1W4 Canada

SCOPE OF WORK

JaBistro Modern Japanese restaurant offers a Japanese bistro style menu where quality and freshness are most important. The project scope entailed new concept design, façade design, dining space, drinks bar, sushi bar and new patio, all designed to reflect the menu.

GOALS AND OBJECTIVES

JaBistro aims to provide an authentic yet modern dining experience that focuses on fresh raw Japanese cuisine. The design goal and objective was to create a calm atmosphere to reflect contemporary Japanese culture appealing to a sophisticated clientele in an urban location.

GOALS ACHIEVED

The layout capitalizes on the narrow space by making the cocktail and raw bar a stage showcasing the freshness of the food being prepared. The existing brick wall accentuated by cove lighting provides a backdrop for the chef. Laminated plywood concealing the ducts frames the bars, while the marble countertop and custom leather dining tables provide a sense of refinement.

BRAND PROMISE

Natural materials were used throughout the space reflecting the fresh menu and the contemporary Japanese culture. Rusted Corten steel used on the façade and framing the banquettes inside calls to mind rusted metal cladding seen on industrial transport ships. Laminated plywood, with a playful striped pattern is a modern twist to traditional Japanese wooden parquetry.

CUSTOMER JOURNEY

Located in the entertainment district of Toronto, the dark façade adapts to its surroundings with a glowing fish logo. A sense of mystery is created as one first approaches the restaurant. The interior is concealed from the outside, but once inside, guests are greeted with a warm and bright interior creating a calm and modern retreat to dine on high quality sushi.

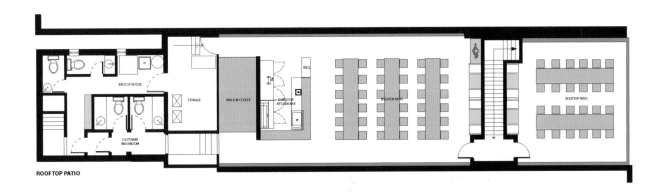

ROOFTOP PATIO

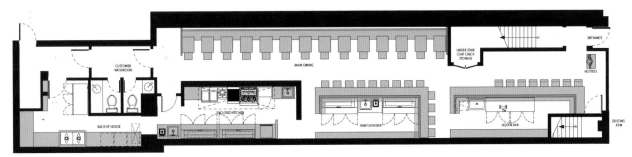

GROUND FLOOR

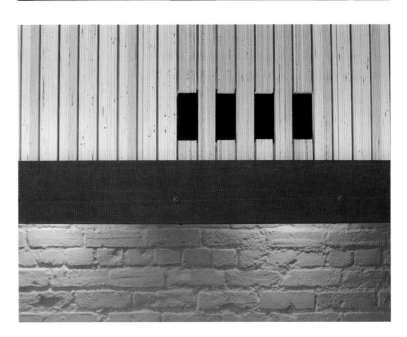

DESIGN FIRM

Dialogue 38, Toronto, ON
Canada

PROJECT DESIGN TEAM
Bennett Lo
Arron Nijhar
Yuju Chang
Sharlene Yuquico
Sunnie Hwang
Jeff Yao

ARCHITECT
Tran Dieu + Associates Inc.,
Toronto, ON Canada
Chi Tran

GENERAL CONTRACTOR
HS Construction Ltd., Toronto, ON
Canada
Jason Lee

OUTSIDE DESIGN CONSULTANTS

Electrical Engineer:
Tran Dieu + Associates, Toronto, ON
Canada

Mechanical Engineer:
Tran Dieu + Associates, Toronto, ON
Canada

SUPPLIERS

Flooring:
Olympia Tile, Toronto, ON Canada

Stone + Tile:
Ciot, Toronto, ON Canada

Lighting:
Contrast Lighting, Toronto, ON
Canada

Signage:
ACL Displayworks, Toronto, ON
Canada

Furniture:
Design Republic, Toronto, ON
Canada

Marin Restaurant & Bar

901 Hennepin Avenue, Minneapolis, MN 55403

SCOPE OF WORK

The goal was to create a new urban restaurant concept transforming the previous space within the Le Meridien Chambers Hotel from stark, contemporary and unapproachable, into a warm, inviting, fine dining destination; to meld a distinct city restaurant with a Northern California lifestyle. Marin was developed into a complete brand: from name, logo, signage, menus and check presentation, to the full interior design.

GOALS ACHIEVED

The space was transformed to maximize square footage, gain additional seats, and create profitable private dining areas. From the full-island outdoor bar, to the high-style street level restaurant, to the library-inspired lower-level lounge, guests have a choice of experiences using California materials throughout.

BRAND PROMISE

The brand promise was built around the idea that guests should leave a restaurant feeling great, not guilty. The experience is a fresh, high quality, chef driven concept in a socially engaging, energized urban environment.

CUSTOMER JOURNEY

Guests are greeted at the bar with a periodic table for hand crafted gin and tonics; or are invited to sit for dinner near the energy of the mosaic wood-fired pizza oven. If cozy cocktails and smaller plates are the goal, the lower-level library lounge is the destination.

BRANDING

Redwood details throughout the space consistently communicate the inspiration for Marin; from the bar and grand entrance wall, to the check presenters—wood-burned with the Marin logo which is introduced and reinforced through all points of contact: menus, water carafes, check presenters and interactive note cards.

ENVIRONMENTAL GRAPHICS

The illuminated logo and branded red awnings dramatically energize the exterior of the corner entrance. Guests are greeted immediately and invited to their choice of seating and experience. On the other side, a grand entrance branded wall welcomes hotel guests into the restaurant.

STORE PLANNING

Marin was built to maximize square footage. There are three distinct spaces that needed to serve different, yet complementary purposes including a complete outdoor bar and patio experience, a fully functional street corner restaurant, and a library-inspired lower level lounge, complete with private dining areas.

FIXTURING

The original staircase in the center was moved to the wall line, opening the restaurant, expanding the bar and adding seats. A wood-burning pizza counter was designed to add theater and energy of a kitchen to the space and the previously non-productive lower level was turned into a lounge with private dining.

FINISHES

The strength and energy of the palette comes from the contrasts including the rich color palette and raw materials integrated into a warm neutral backdrop. Rugs, pillows, and chair fabrics complement but never match, resulting in an effect that is instantly approachable and warm.

LIGHTING

Lighting was the key and the warm gold tones needed to shine through in all day parts. Well-placed, dimmable, warm LED lights, combined with an abundance of natural candlelight achieved this effect. The illuminated artisan glass columns finish the space with intimacy.

VISUAL MERCHANDISING

The logo was created to communicate the DNA of the brand: fresh, farm-to-table fine dining. This inspired the high-style rooster logo finished with contemporary lettering. Each consumer touch point was considered and branded with the fresh and stylish Marin identity.

SUSTAINABILITY

Redwood from fallen trees in Northern California was used in the bar, the check presenters and burl wood was used on main focal walls. Artisans from both Minneapolis and Northern California contributed to the design from artisan glass to wood details.

SALES TECHNOLOGY

To ensure the interconnected spaces of Marin are being monitored and attended, each hostess has an iPad to stay current with of the continuous flow of patrons. To encourage guests to stay in touch with Marin online, take-away business cards are stationed at the hostess stand.

DESIGN FIRM
Shea, Inc., Minneapolis, MN

PROJECT DESIGN TEAM
David Shea, Architect
Amanda Nelson, Designer
Jeremy Nelson, Architect
Tanya Spaulding, Principal
Michelle Brandenburg, Designer
Heidi Kunes, Productions Manager
Peter Moe, Productions Director

STORE DESIGN TEAM
Craig Bentdahl, Owner
Mike Rakun, Executive Chef

ARCHITECT
Shea, Inc., Minneapolis, MN

GENERAL CONTRACTOR
Zeman Construction, Minneapolis, MN
Mark and David Zeman

SUPPLIERS
GAR Products, Lakewood, NJ
ISA, Toronto, ON Canada
BGD Companies, Minneapolis, MN
Architex, Northbrook, IL
Wood Goods, Luke, WI
Little Blind Spot, Hopkins, MN
Marquis Custom Seating,
Minneapolis, MN
Hickory Chair, Minneapolis, MN
Cyrus Carpets, Bloomington, MN
Madeline Weinrib Showroom, New
York, NY
Emeco, Hanover, PA
Innovations, New York, NY
Mayer Fabrics, Indianapolis, IN
Pollack, New York, NY
SML, Carlaw, ON Canada
Gemini, Cannon Falls, MN
Trelloge, Ferrill, Minneapolis, MN

Richmond Centre Dining Terrace

Richmond Centre, 6551 No.3 Road, Richmond, BC V6Y 2B6 Canada

SCOPE OF WORK

The renovation converted Richmond Centre's second level Multiplex Theatre into an open-concept Dining Terrace. From the beginning, Richmond Centre set out to design an environmentally friendly, contemporary dining terrace for their shoppers.

GOALS AND OBJECTIVES

The renovation planning and execution goal was to create an urban, modern and environmentally conscious design. The mission was to evoke a restaurant quality environment elevating the mall dining experience to a new level with a tenant mix offering a combination of national chains and local restaurateurs.

GOALS ACHIEVED

In working with each tenant the food court design team controlled the aesthetics from materials, lighting, menu graphics and brand identity to ensure a clean visual vocabulary was executed in keeping with the overall look of the Dining Terrace. The space features many unique design elements including reclaimed British Columbia wood tables, orange, green, charcoal and grey chairs of recycled PET bottles and original music to capture the ambiance.

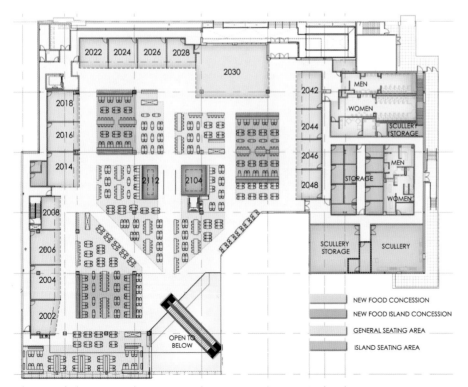

BRAND PROMISE

The brand promise is to provide an affordable, high quality and healthy fast-service dining option in the heart of the Richmond Centre. The Dining Terrace assembles a variety of conventional and new-to-market food offerings in a slick urban environment. An environmental commitment is made to Cadillac Fairview's "Green at Work" program by introducing dishware, flatware and scullery service as an alternative to plastic dishes and cutlery, dramatically reducing waste.

CUSTOMER JOURNEY

An escalator transports visitors from the ground level to the food court's 2nd level location. All walls around the escalator were demolished to promote full open vistas. A wood ceiling projects from the Dining Terrace over the escalators into the mall common area teasing visitors to explore the upper level. Featured are specialized seating for select tenants, stand-alone kiosks for others, and an overall sleek modern design.

BRANDING

A design review committee oversaw the menu graphics and brand identity of each tenant to ensure a cool and contemporary visual vocabulary in keeping with the overall look. Each tenant underwent a revitalization of their brand image including the inline tenants and stand-alone kiosks.

ENVIRONMENTAL GRAPHICS

Each tenant from the national chains to the local favorites underwent a revitalization of their brand image. The results are striking and noteworthy food units that have significant design merit in their own right.

STORE PLANNING

The varied seating layouts support a dynamic customer experience. The dining terrace boasts specialized seating for select tenants, stand-alone kiosks for others, and a sleek modern style across all. Two freestanding island locations were created to promote a more interactive and interesting traffic flow, avoiding a typical "run of retailers."

FIXTURING

High quality merchandising is achieved via curated food presentation that was outlined in the Tenant Design Manual and subject to Design Committee review. All fixtures were designed in keeping with an urban aesthetic, yet highly durable to withstand the rigors of heavy traffic.

FINISHES

The food court entry has a wood ceiling. Porcelain mosaic tiles clad the low walls (bar counters); the columns and floor are covered with larger porcelain tiles. All fixtures are custom millwork and include long communal tables of white quartz and stainless steel. Etched glass was used for partitions separating each tenant.

LIGHTING

A new double-level clerestory to the right of the escalators saturates the food court with natural daylight. To preserve the natural light and ensure an environmentally sustainable mission, seven LED skylights with daylight intensity LED cove lights were positioned throughout the space.

VISUAL MERCHANDISING

Perhaps the greatest achievement is how high the bar has been raised in terms of tenant design and presentation. Strong emphasis for each tenant to showcase their food and merchandise was enforced in carefully crafted design criteria that ensure a singular vision is embraced by all tenants, resulting in a harmonious blend of national and local restaurateurs.

SUSTAINABILITY

In adherence to Cadillac Fairview's Green initiatives program, recycled/reclaimed wood and recycled chairs were used. To preserve natural light seven LED skylights with LED cove lights were positioned throughout the space. The skylights have been equipped with daylight intensity LED cove lights to mimic natural light. Hot water heats the air as it passes through the space and is thus cooled and saving energy cooling.

DESIGN FIRM
GH+A, Montreal, QC Canada

PROJECT DESIGN TEAM
Denis Gervais, Partner in Charge
Joni Vallon, Project Director
Lily Yuan, Senior Designer
Anicka Nault, Designer
Charmie Seo, Architectural Technician

ARCHITECT
Abbarch Architecture Inc., Vancouver, BC Canada
Daryl Hutchison, Associate Principal

GENERAL CONTRACTOR
PCL Construction Westcoast Inc., Richmond, BC Canada
Bonifacio Enriquez, Project Manager

OUTSIDE DESIGN CONSULTANTS
Architect:
Abbarch Architecture Inc., Vancouver, BC Canada

General Contractor:
PCL Construction, Richmond, BC Canada

Landscape Architect:
Hapa Collective, Vancouver, BC Canada

Lighting Consultants:
Gabriel Mackinnon, Ottawa, ON Canada

Structural Engineers:
RJC Consulting, Vancouver, BC Canada

Mechanical Engineers:
Bycar Engineering Ltd., Surrey, BC Canada

Sprinklers Engineers:
Tru-Line Technologies Ltd., Port Moody, BC Canada

Electrical Engineers:
S+A Falcon, Burnaby, BC Canada

Geo-Technical Engineer:
Levelton Consultants Ltd., Richmond, BC Canada

SUPPLIERS
Furniture:
Klaus, Toronto, ON Canada
ISA International Inc., Toronto, ON Canada

Millwork:
JSV Architectural Veneering & Millwork Inc., Port Coquitlam, BC Canada

Lighting:
Gabriel Mackinnon, Ottawa, ON Canada

Tiles (low walls and counters):
Ciot, Montreal, QC Canada

Tiles (columns):
Centura, Montreal, QC Canada

Tiles (flooring):
Stone Tile International Inc., Toronto, ON Canada
Olympia Tile, Montreal, QC Canada

Accoustic Tiles:
Armstrong, Lancaster, PA

Reclaimed Wood:
Live Edge Design, Duncan, BC Canada
Coast Ecotimber, Vancouver, BC Canada

Photography:
Ed White Photographics, Vancouver, BC Canada

GH+A

An international creative retail design firm with BIG BOLD IDEAS!

Founded in 1985 with an exclusive focus on retail design, GH+A today employs 75 creative designers and retail thinkers in its Montreal and Detroit studios.

Our expertise in redesigning shopping centres, combined with our multiple award-winning store design portfolio, grants us a unique position of privilege in the retail universe. It provides us with priceless insight into the world of the retailer, as well as that of the landlord. It makes us different.

We create exciting new store concepts and define the retail experience in close colaboration with our clients, remaining faithful to the brand mission. In taking the time to understand our client's business and strategic objectives, we design stores that resonate with the customer and improve the bottom line for the retailer.

It's one thing to walk through a store, it's quite another to experience a store. At GH+A, we reinforce the connection between the brand and consumer so it becomes something that shoppers will remember, that special something that makes them say: "Let's go back!".

International Currency Exchange

Aéropostale

B.Spoke

CORE

Get inside our creative minds...
Visit our website and follow us!

ghadesign.com
514.843.5812

Kung Pao Wok

Richmond Centre Dining Terrace, 6551 No. 3 Road, Richmond, BC V6Y 2B6 Canada

SCOPE OF WORK

Kung Pao Wok is a Chinese food vendor located in the newly renovated food court at Richmond Centre in British Columbia and the designers were asked to create an entirely new concept design for the project.

GOALS AND OBJECTIVES

The goal of the design was to create a fast food experience that would visually set Kung Pao Wok apart from other food vendors. It was also a design objective and client's need to maintain traditional Chinese symbolism throughout.

GOALS ACHIEVED

Taking advantage of its corner location, the design features a custom mosaic wall mural that promotes traditional Chinese values of strength, prosperity, and good fortune. Striking graphics and bold colors were used throughout the walls and counter to allow the food vendor to visually stand out in the food court. The design highlights a custom mosaic wall depicting a red Chinese dragon flying through a bright blue sky, hinting at Kung Pao Wok's cultural values.

BRAND PROMISE

The design reflects the food offerings of traditional Chinese cooking but with a modern twist. The use of bright colors and bold graphics suggest a casual and fun food experience.

CUSTOMER JOURNEY

As a powerful symbol of strength and good fortune, the dragon draws visitors to the vendor with the help of splashes of deep red. Symbolic dragon pearls contain menu offerings that are carefully integrated into the mosaic mural. Lastly, illuminated red clouds rendered on the counter face further symbolize good fortune in traditional Chinese culture.

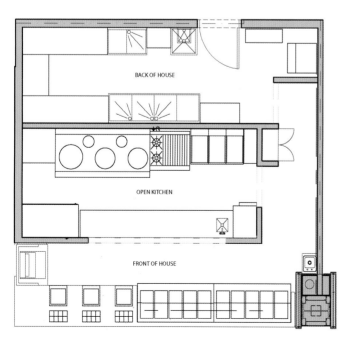

DESIGN FIRM
Dialogue 38, Toronto, ON
Canada

PROJECT DESIGN TEAM
Bennett Lo
Jeff Yao
Yuju Chang

ARCHITECT
Urban Design Group, Vancouver,
BC Canada
Paul Chiu

GENERAL CONTRACTOR
Flaming Wok International Inc.,
Development Division, Richmond, BC
Canada
Ivan Cirjak

OUTSIDE DESIGN CONSULTANTS

Electrical Engineer:
**Smith + Anderson Falcon
Engineering,** Vancouver, BC Canada

Mechanical Engineer:
Bycar Engineering Ltd., Surrey, BC
Canada

SUPPLIERS

Flooring:
Daltile, Vancouver, BC Canada

Stone + Tile:
Modern Mixed Tiles, Toronto, ON

Canada
Ciot, Toronto, ON Canada

Lighting:
Contrast Lighting, Toronto, ON
Canada

Signage:
ACL Displayworks, Toronto, ON
Canada

Nespresso Boutique Bar

159 Cumberland Street, Toronto, ON M5R 1A2 Canada

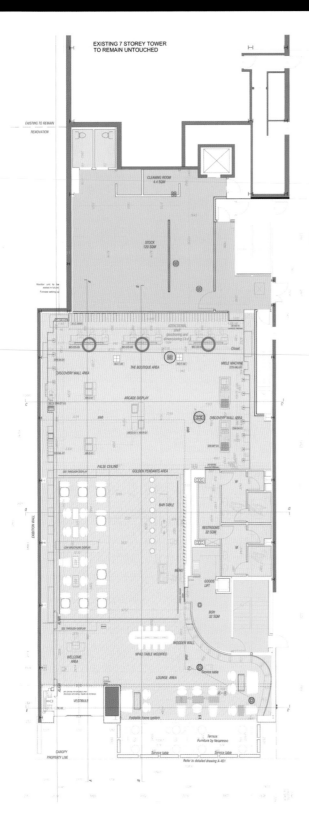

SCOPE OF WORK

A boutique bar design inside a former cinema: architecture (new facade, completely renovated spaces and volumes), interior design (layout, custom made furniture, choice of loose furniture, special installation, ceiling and flooring design, finishes), and lighting design.

GOALS AND OBJECTIVES

The designers created a highly recognizable new place in the city of Toronto for coffee tasting and purchasing, space where quality design meets quality coffee offering customers the ultimate coffee experience. The project aspires to become a major commercial point of reference and a new contemporary architectural landmark.

GOALS ACHIEVED

The former cinema has been transformed: outside the transparent facade lets people get involved to what's going on inside; at night this architectural element works as a beacon to draw attention to the boutique. The format of the bar offers multiple options to enjoy slowly or quickly and allows clientele to get in touch with a very rich world of values.

BRAND PROMISE

This flagship café and retail space strengthens Nespresso's presence in Toronto and awareness of the brand's commitment to quality and excellence. The challenge was to create an airy and dynamic café that invites guests to experience the attainable luxury that characterizes the firm's products. An atmosphere of quality and service encourages customers to journey to the boutique to learn more and ultimately bring the experience to their own home.

CUSTOMER JOURNEY

The boutique bar houses two main commercial areas: a first zone (bar) where multiple option of coffee enjoying are provided: quick counter tasting area with tables for small groups, Npad tables with stools and internet connectivity; and a lounge area with armchairs and sofas for longer stays and meetings. The boutique has multiple selling zones for coffee, machines and accessories located at the end of the space.

BRANDING

Impactful, bright and warm, the space provides the perfect environment to experience a world of values. Different areas offer customers a specific zone to enjoy the brand their own way.

ENVIRONMENTAL GRAPHICS

A well-studied corporate image reflects consistent communication through visual, light boxes, and displays. The world-renowned N monogram is a recognizable mark and the wide range of eye-catching colors present a coffee Grand Crus.

STORE PLANNING

The welcome zone is an impactful double-height area that leads to the bar, defined by a suspended installation of metal tubes. The lounge area on the right is connected to the outdoor terrace; the boutique is located at the back of the space under a lower ceiling.

FIXTURING

Focus on product is a key element of the design: recognizable branding, and sleeve boxes for coffee capsules play a main role in the boutique area. On the wall behind the counters, a variety of Grand Crus is colorfully displayed. Machines and accessories have dedicated displays with specific furniture elements with self-illuminated or backlit displays, shelves, libraries or freestanding modules.

FINISHES

The boutique area is recognizable for the use of rosewood veneer, while a lighter oak veneer is the key finishing choice for the bar. Smooth Corian surfaces mark the main customer surfaces, while premium fabrics and leather are used for all seating.

LIGHTING

A wise mix of recessed downlights in ceiling coves, suspended light fixture and backlit/self illuminated furniture elements combine to create a warm atmosphere with diffuse general lighting to focus attention on the merchandise.

VISUAL MERCHANDISING

Display approaches exemplify Nespresso's commitment to everyday luxury in all aspects of their product experience. Products are shown in an eye-catching way to attract customers.

SUSTAINABILITY

All materials are FSC certified. LED lighting has been implemented in all Nespresso lighting concepts. For the past few years, a coffee capsules collecting station for recycling has been utilized as a standard furniture element in stores.

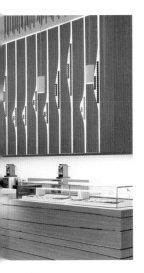

DESIGN FIRM
Parisotto + Formenton
Architects, Milano, Italy

PROJECT DESIGN TEAM
Aldo Parisotto
Massimo Formenton
Francesca Squadrelli
Marco Manicone

STORE DESIGN TEAM
Senka Perc, Project Manager
Matteo Bressanin, International Retail Manager

ARCHITECT
Parisotto + Formenton Architects, Milano, Italy
Antigone Acconci

GENERAL CONTRACTOR
Structure Corp., Toronto, ON Canada
Nilton Tavares

SUPPLIERS
Furniture:
Essequattro S.p.A., Grisignano di Zocco, Italy

Lighting:
Regency Lighting, Chatsworth, CA

Photography:
A-Frame Incorporated, Toronto, ON Canada
Ben Rahn

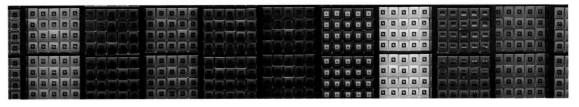

t.boutique & t.bar

Lange Reihe 68/70, 20099 Hamburg, Germany

SCOPE OF WORK

The project entailed creating a new place for tea lovers—a specialty/concept store for a new tea brand. Therefore, a store area (approx. 90 sq.m.) in St. Georg—an upcoming district of Hamburg—was completely renovated and redesigned.

GOALS AND OBJECTIVES

The goal was to create a unique and chainable fusion of a modern teashop and tea bar for the new tea brand t and t´s strapline "hand-picked happiness"; a unique place to go for enjoyment, conversation, relaxing and shopping. The product tea comes alive in three distinct, harmoniously merging areas: t.bar (drinking and eating), t.boutique (shopping) and t.school (tea tasting seminars).

GOALS ACHIEVED

t.boutique & t.bar is a perfect staging for the tea brand t and a great place for tea lovers where Asian tea tradition melts with modern European tea consuming habits. Open spaces, brightness and friendliness characterize the interior. Colors and materials reflect the brand and its values: high quality, modernity and naturalness.

BRAND PROMISE

t.boutique & t.bar is a unique world of tea under one roof, offering all natural, high class, handpicked teas and innovative tea related products.

CUSTOMER JOURNEY

Looking, smelling, touching, tasting and shopping: The customer is invited to explore a modern world of tea—with all senses and with no limits or restrictions.

BRANDING

Purity, simplicity, exclusivity and weightlessness of tea—the interior reflects all aspects of the brand "t". All furniture and materials are—as tea—natural. The color concept matches the color code of the brand "t." Individually hand made decorative items and furniture underline the brand's slogan, "handpicked happiness."

ENVIRONMENTAL GRAPHICS

To attract the passers-by "t" is presented in the form of a huge letter on the shop window. Although small, the store is clearly structured in three different areas. Due to the concept of transparency t.boutique and t.bar are clearly separated but seem to melt together—everything can be easily seen from either side. A floor color code guides clientele to the t.school located in the basement.

STORE PLANNING

The customer is immediately welcomed at the t.bar situated at the entrance. Next to the bar the journey starts at the tea exploration wall. From here the customer explores—either guided or on his own—to the t.boutique and t.school.

FIXTURING

To underscore the concept of weightlessness, all shelves are directly fixed to the walls and made of thin steel. All products are displayed to have full effect. With the help of small magnets, paper cards with product and price information can be easily affixed.

FINISHES

All materials are natural: linoleum floor, wood and steel furniture, covered lighting partially covered in silk fabric, and handmade ottomans. The key customer touchpoint is the tea exploration wall. On big wooden shelves the tea is presented in small steel-cups hidden under glass vases, that once opened, release the beautiful flavors.

LIGHTING

The use of lighting serves to separate store areas. LED technology in the shelves of the tea exploration wall highlight the main customer touch-point, fabric covered lamps provide a warm atmosphere for the seating areas. A ceiling box construction contains the bright lighting for the bar area, ceiling spotlights stage the commercial products.

VISUAL MERCHANDISING

At t.boutique & t.bar the customer is able to explore all products with all senses—looking, touching, smelling, tasting—and ultimately, purchasing.

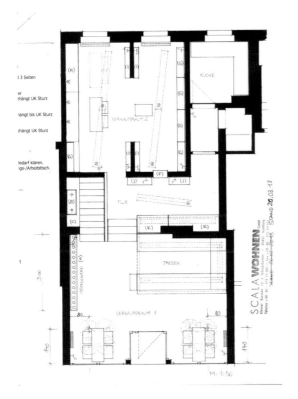

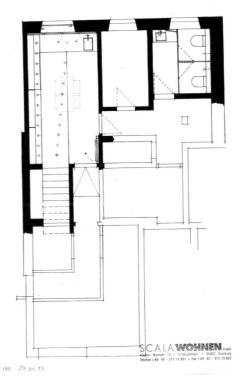

DESIGN FIRM

t.lovers GmbH,
Hamburg, Germany

PROJECT DESIGN TEAM
Eva Bˆhmer-Krause
Martin Sasse
Silke Sasse

ARCHITECT
she-architekten, Hamburg, Germany
Stephan Schrick

OUTSIDE DESIGN CONSULTANTS
Interior Design:
SCALA Wohnen GmbH, Hamburg,
Germany
Volker Hartmann

Lighting:
PG Licht GmbH, Winsen (Luhe),
Germany
Jens Ambros

Graphics, etc.:
t.lovers GmbH, Hamburg, Germany
Silke Sasse

SUPPLIERS
Whlke Mbelmanufaktur GmbH,
Stuhr/Brinkum, Germany

Telstra Retail Store of the Future

Melbourne Central, Melbourne, VIC 3000, Australia

SCOPE OF WORK

Telstra required a new store concept to achieve higher levels of customer advocacy and changes being made inside the business. This included: a new operating strategy, defining a new customer and staff experience, creating an in-store support system, and creating a store environment that evolves in response to customer/staff feedback and technology.

GOALS AND OBJECTIVES

The project goal was to create a new store environment that would support Telstra's key business strategy, "to improve customer advocacy—change the way customers talk about Telstra." The project objectives were: make customer/staff behavior-centric, an interactive store environment, efficient/timely service, a unique shopping experience, an attractive workplace with high caliber/knowledgeable staff, a flexible fit-out, and cost effective construction and roll-out.

GOALS ACHIEVED

The store provides customers the opportunity to create their own experience with interactive LED screen entertainment, 'Educate, Test and Decide' zone, mobile docks and self-manage facilities. Staff is supported by a store toolkit enabling them to create individual customer experiences. Products are arranged by brand with entire kits for "connecting customer's worlds."

BRAND PROMISE

Brand promise: "It's how we connect"—Helping customers connect; "Improve the way people live and work"—core brand attributes . . . talked about every day. The colors used in Telstra's visual brand expression allow them to connect to a spectrum of different Australian customer demographics. Bringing the brand to life, a tangible brand experience for customers and staff: connecting Telstra to the community; connecting customers and staff; connecting customers' lives with humility and simplicity

CUSTOMER JOURNEY

Customers are attracted to the openness, warmth and humility of the store. They move about intuitively without the sense of process or protocols. They are free to explore products; self-educate and discover new technologies and products choosing to be unaided or assisted.

BRANDING

The focus is not on branding through signage, environmental graphics and brand colors. It is translating the brand into a customer experience enabling effective connection with Telstra staff and interactive technologies with settings and tools of choice. Its agility and scalability enables a consistent and holistic brand experience.

ENVIRONMENTAL GRAPHICS

Environmental graphics are replaced by an interactive brand experience. The environment offers digital and interactive screens that visually connect the Telstra brand and support the business in developing an integrated omni channel experience. Planning for intuitive navigation negates the need for wayfinding.

STORE PLANNING

Open, organic planning and optional settings provide a flexible, supportive "toolkit" for staff to engage with customers how and where customers are most comfortable: standing, leaning, perching or sitting, for fast or slow, easy or complex situations. Real products and digital content means staff remain with customers.

FIXTURING

The fixture kit: tracks, poles, panels and cable containment units enable easy reconfiguration of the store layout. They provide for total branded product stories, physical and virtual at a single point. Staff can flex the kit to suit different offers and events and refresh the customer experience.

FINISHES

Natural and relaxed tones and tactile textures were used to support and highlight products and technologies, allowing brand colors to ignite within digital content. Premium fabric was used on the surface of the consulting tables to give a quality experience to the customer when unpackaged products are presented.

LIGHTING

LED lighting with integrated control panels allows one-touch changes for different times, days and events. Track lighting allows change of light positions to suit flexible dynamic layouts, while feature highlighting pulls the eye to key products. Warm light temperature supports the materiality and brand.

VISUAL MERCHANDISING

A "cellar" concept presents a curated display that demonstrates the full product range, providing inspiration and theatre while eliminating the need for back of house storage space.

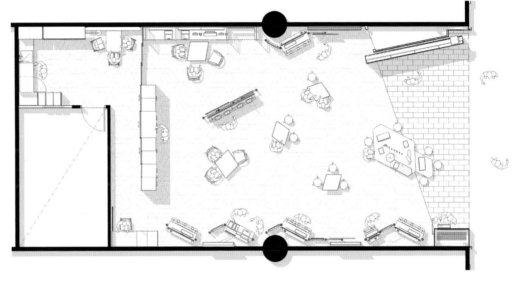

DESIGN FIRM
Geyer, Melbourne, VIC, Australia

PROJECT DESIGN TEAM
Rebecca Daff
Robyn Lindsey
Tim Giles
Tom Reid

GENERAL CONTRACTOR
Cara Interior Project Management,
Melbourne, VIC, Australia
Steve Burfurd

OUTSIDE DESIGN CONSULTANTS

Lighting:
2B Designed, Melbourne, VIC, Australia
David Bird

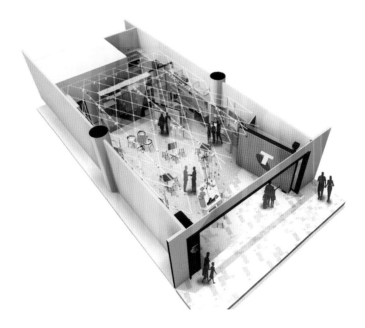

Light that sparks creativity,
fuels imagination.

That's Amerlux
at work.

Amerlux lighting creates environments that foster
productivity—it's no wonder more businesses are
turning to our linear lighting solutions.

Discover how Amerlux lights up success at
www.amerlux.com.

Passion. Power. Performance.

AT&T Store of the Future

1025 Lenox Park Blvd., Atlanta, GA 30319

SCOPE OF WORK

The scope of work involved the strategic evolution of AT&T's retail experience into a brand new store prototype and breaks the mold of traditional telecom retailing by shifting focus onto the experience that mobile products enable in our daily lives, instead of on the technology itself. The new store design will be rolling out in approximately 14 locations.

GOALS AND OBJECTIVES

The new store concept builds on the momentum of AT&T's Michigan Ave. Flagship store (2012), but designed to scale into the rest of the company-owned retail store portfolio and create a new store experience that would be an expression of the evolving AT&T brand, building customer loyalty through exploration, education and AT&T's innovative products and services. The design is intended to be flexible, fun and approachable to feel fresh and relevant to the customer.

GOALS ACHIEVED

This project breaks the mold of traditional telecom retailing, showcasing how mobile devices are integrated into our everyday lives, not just on the device itself! The store experience is designed to "humanize technology. Visually rich product stories come to life in the flexible "Experience Pavilions" zone while the "Community Tables" provide a platform for AT&T to showcase curated collections of apps, accessories and devices. The "Learning Tables" and mobile sales staff help to turn transactions into interactions and change the paradigm of the large fixed cash wraps of yesteryear.

BRAND PROMISE

At the core of AT&T's mission, vision, and brand personality, is a commitment to deliver the future that is relevant, approachable and friendly. AT&T's tagline, "Rethink Possible" is a call to action that is open and limitless; a mix of optimism, energy and enthusiasm, grounded with a sense of warmth and approachability. The designers created a place where this promise comes to life, a place where the line between technology and humanity blurs.

CUSTOMER JOURNEY

The journey starts outside with expansive views into the store. Inside the journey is designed to be open, inviting and organized, creating a visit that is intuitive, effortless and engaging. The store has four primary areas: Experience Pavilion where customers get inspired to play with the products, Community Zone at the center for curated stories and customer connections, and finally the Explore Walls and Solution Center.

BRANDING

Overall, our goal was to create a physical manifestation of the AT&T Brand that "humanizes" the technology and experience of shopping for a mobile device and service through open and intuitive planning, creating places for customers to have face-to-face interactions and provide relevant, engaging and interactive product experiences.

ENVIRONMENTAL GRAPHICS

One of the unique aspects of the new design is the integrated video technology that is woven throughout the entire design. Digital media is used to create a rich and dynamic ambient "brand canvas" that visually stiches together different areas while humanizing the overall experience through textural environmental motion graphics.

STORE PLANNING

The overall store layout has been designed to be open, inviting and organized, creating a customer journey that is intuitive, effortless and fun. Shopping, service and experience zones are defined through hard and soft floor surfaces, open and closed ceiling elements and differing levels of lighting.

FIXTURING

New fixtures were developed using a combination of wood, white solid surface and thick acrylic elements. They allow flexibility through movement, magnetic panels and modular acrylic pads for product storytelling and interactive experiences. Variety of scale and organization create a comfortable and communal shopping experience.

FINISHES

Finishes were driven by the intention to design for humanity, while staying true to AT&T's technology presence. This was achieved through the warmth of reclaimed teak wood juxtaposed with crisp white modern fixtures and glass elements all balanced with pops of AT&T's brand color orange as furniture accents.

Merchandise Plan

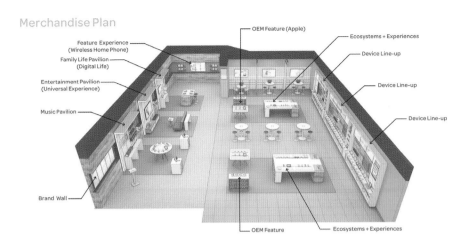

- OEM Feature (Apple)
- Ecosystems + Experiences
- Feature Experience (Wireless Home Phone)
- Device Line-up
- Family Life Pavilion (Digital Life)
- Device Line-up
- Entertainment Pavilion (Universal Experience)
- Music Pavilion
- Device Line-up
- Brand Wall
- OEM Feature
- Ecosystems + Experiences

DESIGN OVERVIEW:

1. Expanded use of large floor fixtures like the "community" tables provide more display capacity in a smaller area allowing for new elements, like the Learning Tables and Experience Pavilions to be incorporated into the design.

2. A greater variety of merchandising and experience zones provides more flexibility and adaptability for a wider array of products.

3. "Solutions Selling" and immersive experience areas deliver extraordinary customer experience.

NOTES

LIGHTING

The lighting creates a warm, comfortable, bright, and fresh atmosphere. Highs and lows in the lighting levels create drama and interest in the Experience Pavilion zone, with more even light in the Community Zone and customer service areas. LED track and recessed heads combine with linear fluorescents to provide the right balance of ambient vs. adjustable lighting.

VISUAL MERCHANDISING

The visual merchandising takes cues from fashion merchandising, creating storytelling moments and lifestyle collections. Experience Pavilions mix residential-styled fixtures, furniture, props and home-inspired elements to humanize the experience. Products are presented as "connected solutions" combining device, accessory and app into a single story.

SUSTAINABILITY

The design used many of the same strategies, materials and systems that helped AT&T's Michigan Ave. Flagship achieve LEED Platinum. The prototype was designed with sustainability in mind. Highlights include an LED lighting package, and the use of reclaimed and regionally sourced, low-VOC materials and fixtures.

SALES TECHNOLOGY

Rethinking the way that customers are assisted by technology throughout the sales process was at the heart of the experience design. Traditional cash wraps were eliminated, replaced with mobile landing stations, café-style Learning Tables, and sit-down lounge areas, all used by iPad armed sales and service staff help to change "transactions into interactions."

DESIGN FIRM
Callison Architecture,
Seattle, WA

PROJECT DESIGN TEAM

Callison Architecture:

Alex Shapleigh, Design Principal
Michelle McCormick, Account Manager
Ryan Gorman, Designer
Mitch Pride, Designer
Travis Brown, Designer
Nguyen Nguyen, Project Architect
Marie Chow, Project Architect
Haley Harrigan-Rottle, Interior Designer
Raquel Gushi, Architectural Staff

AT&T:

Mike Chisholm, Executive Director, Retail Real Estate & Store Design
Lourdes Burson, Director, Store Design
Mary Jenkins, Executive Director, Retail Technology
Christie Beals, Director, Retail Technology
Tim Johnson, Senior Technical Director, CDI/Retail Technology
Maria Simpson, Executive Director, MarCom
Jonathan Lander, Director, MarCom
Vickie Berry, Executive Director, Corporate Real Estate
Jason Anderson, Construction Management

ARCHITECT

Callison Architecture, Seattle, WA
Alex Shapleigh, Design Principal

GENERAL CONTRACTOR

US Communications, Alpharetta, GA
David Williamson

OUTSIDE DESIGN CONSULTANTS

Digital Experiences:

Maxmedia, Atlanta, GA
Jeff Doud, Executive Creative Director

Visual Merchandising:

The Integer Group, Dallas, TX
Mark Mayland, VP, Creative Director

Lighting Design:

Oculus Lighting, Santa Monica, CA
Archit Jain

Engineering:

Δdifica Case Engineering, St. Louis, MO
David Case

SUPPLIERS

Fixture Fabrication:

RCS Innovations, Milwaukee, WI
Midwest Store Fixtures, University Park, IL

Merchandising Displays:

Impact Displays Group, LLC, Carlstadt, NJ

Carpet:

Shaw Contract, Atlanta, GA

Raised Flooring:

Haworth, Seattle, WA

Lighting Supply:

Amerlux, Fairfield, NJ
Grainger, Forest Park, GA

Reclaimed Teak:

TerraMai, White City, OR

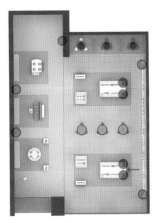

Customer Interaction & Transaction Points

American Express Centurion Lounge

McCarran International Airport, Las Vegas, NV

SCOPE OF WORK

The expansive scope of work included: schematic exploration; prototypical design; experience programming; concept development; space planning; experience design; interior and exterior design; colors, materials and finishes; architectural services, and more.

GOALS AND OBJECTIVES

The team sought to create a truly unique, differentiated travel experience that delivered on the brand promise and embodied American Express' commitment to the art of service. The physical environment needed to reward members while providing an integrated platform for brand expression and engagement.

GOALS ACHIEVED

Iconic design furnishings and multisensory elements are pulled together in a modern, memorable environment that transports guests away from the concourse's hectic atmosphere and rewards them with unexpected services and amenities. Luxurious finishes combine with intuitive, personalized service to elevate the experience and intensify brand relevance.

BRAND PROMISE

The American Express brand is committed to world-class service and extraordinary experiences. The brand devotes itself to service that anticipates, satisfies, and exceeds customers' evolving needs. American Express is constantly adapting to offer customers opportunities to achieve extraordinary experiences, big and small.

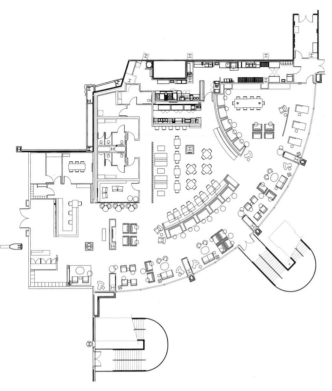

CUSTOMER JOURNEY

Iconic blue doors and a living green wall beckon guests into the Lounge. Inside, the Lounge offers endless opportunities for card members to relax, unwind, and experience the art of service. Flexible seating arrangements and exceptional amenities cater to business travelers, travel enthusiasts and families alike.

DESIGN FIRM
Big Red Rooster,
Columbus, OH

CLIENT
American Express Company

PROJECT DESIGN TEAM
Aaron Spiess
Diane Rambo
Don Hasulak, AIA
Beth Dorsey
Vicki Eickelberger
David Denniston
Kathy Kline
Jenine Monks
Elaine Roberts
John Hamlett

STORE DESIGN TEAM
Troy Williams
Lisa Skilling-Belmond
Angela Cheung

GENERAL CONTRACTOR
Turner Construction Company,
Columbus, Ohio

OUTSIDE DESIGN CONSULTANTS
MEP:
Larson Binkley, Kansas City, MO

A/V Consultant:
The Integration Factory, Rockledge, FL

SUPPLIERS

Flooring:
Hard & Soft Surface
Stone Source, Chicago, IL
Kaswell, Framingham, MA
Caccese Collection, New York, NY

Lighting:
MOOOi, Netherlands
JGoode Designs, Castle Rock, CO

Furniture:
Vitra Voltage Inc., Cincinnati, OH
Knoll CIC, Columbus, OH
Mike Magill, New York, NY
John Houshmand, New York, NY
FatBoy, Coppell, TX

Millwork:
Western Millwork, Inc., Phoenix, AZ

Paint & Finishes:
A Touch of Venetian Art, Elmwood Park, IL
Scuffmaster, Columbus, OH
Benjamin Moore, Chicago, IL

Plastic Laminates:
Formica, Cincinnati, OH

Special Finishes:
Elmwood Reclaimed Timber,
Peculiar, MS

Amuneal Manufacturing Corp.,
Philadelphia, PA
Pulp Studio, Los Angeles, CA
Color Text Inc., Columbus, OH

Wallcoverings:
Maharam, Columbus, OH
Carnegie, Cincinnati, OH
Koroseal, Columbus, OH

Fabric Finishes:
Maharam, Columbus, OH
Knoll, East Greenville, PA
Carnegie, Rockville Centre, NY
Opuzen, Los Angeles
Silver Threads, Columbus, OH

Other features:
**GSky Plant Systems Inc./Living
Green Wall,** Delray Beach, FL
12.29: Custom Scent, New York, NY

Rock Paper Photo:
Custom Photography, New York, NY

Optic Nerve:
Media Wall Artifacts, Columbus, OH

Iconic Dog Brand Artwork:
Creative Cabinets Ltd., Lancaster, OH
Solar Imaging, Columbus, OH
Big Red Rooster, Columbus, OH

Qi Master Reflexology

Westfield Doncaster, 619 Doncaster Road, Doncaster, Victoria 3108, Australia

SCOPE OF WORK

A reflexology-specific store is a new genre of service in the Australian retail sector. To introduce this service the store had to be edgy, punchy and bold, yet recognizably Chinese in its appearance emphasizing contemporary Chinese references and materiality. Re-branding, graphics, store design, styling and brand direction were needed including logo, graphic language, and printed collateral. Store design, retail experience and aesthetic were extended, fine-tuning the qualitative experience on offer.

GOALS AND OBJECTIVES

The store was designed to challenge public perception and expectation of a shopping center Chinese massage store creating a moody, gallery-like space that offered an insight into contemporary Chinese culture and an ancient therapeutic practice. The space is enchanting and theatrical, enticing the passersby to come in. The dialectics of privacy/voyeurism and prospect/refuge were considered alongside service and customer comfort.

GOALS ACHIEVED

Curated with contemporary Chinese imagery, bamboo poles and brass in the form of a giant sink and bespoke light fittings, the space is imbued with an overriding sense of contemporary Chinese cool. The end product is a vibrant, dramatic and immersive point of difference to its competitors that captivates the passerby. Users are afforded the luxury of a self-contained, semi-private-oasis, enabling a voyeuristic tidbit of engagement.

BRAND PROMISE

The brand promise is one of cultural authenticity and by inference a more authentic reflexology service. The use of strong graphic imagery, and associative materiality celebrate the ceremonial aspect of the treatment. All elements collude to create a sense of oriental luxury, indulgence and retreat.

CUSTOMER JOURNEY

The consumer experience is designed to embraces typically hidden but culturally and ritualistically significant aspects of the service beginning with the dramatic landscape that transports the user from the suburban shopping mall to a dream-like place. The ritual filling of the soaking tub introduces water as an element in the journey. Curved pod walls and linen curtains cocoon the customer in a space that allows a filtered view out yet offers privacy within.

BRANDING

Designed in conjunction with the store and with similar aspirations, the logo is a stylized Chinese signature seal with both Chinese and Latin script. Manifested as a neon sign on the shop-front, the allusion to a contemporary Asian city is reiterated.

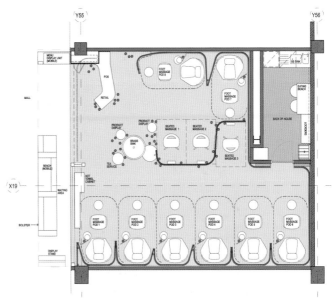

ENVIRONMENTAL GRAPHICS

Graphics are key to the immersive experience. A collection of images with a contemporary Chinese theme populates the walls. Since reflexology is a relatively unknown practice in Australia, a foot reflexology chart within each pod educates the customer on reflexology principles.

STORE PLANNING

Vibrant graphic pod walls line the outer perimeter overlooking a centrally controlled landscape of natural elements (bamboo and water) in a theatrical-set like fashion. Customers select a distinctive pod of their choice, the curtain is drawn and the pampering begins.

FIXTURING

Water for the filling of the soaking tubs is delivered from the ceiling via a brass tube operated by an industrial utilitarian turn knob. The combination of "blingy" brass (gold being auspicious in Chinese culture) with the industrial fitting is unique and playful.

LIGHTING

The ambiance of the moody space is punctuated with vivid hotspots illuminating the imagery on the curved pod walls and the bamboo forest. Strip lighting along the pod walls highlight the wall curvature while the artisan crafted neon logo on the shop-front references Hong Kong street signs.

VISUAL MERCHANDISING

A series of tiered circular shelves provide a platform upon which various tasks are performed or a retail offering presented. A dedicated Chinese tea service station delivers freshly brewed green tea, while another houses a variety of traditional Chinese herbs, freshly mixed based on the customer's selection.

SUSTAINABILITY

Flooring is linoleum, a natural product made from 97% natural raw materials. The bamboo is Australian grown and the plywood is recycled. Low VOC paints and water based environmentally friendly finishes are applied to all joinery. Local artisans made the bespoke brass light fittings, brass sink, and neon logo.

DESIGN FIRM
Pinto Tuncer Pty Ltd.,
Melbourne, VIC Australia

PROJECT AND STORE DESIGN TEAM
Ilker Tuncer
Gerard Pinto
Emily Li

ARCHITECT
Pinto Tuncer, Melbourne, VIC Australia
Ilker Tuncer

GENERAL CONTRACTOR
Osmo Construction, Melbourne, VIC Australia
Sunny Ho

OUTSIDE DESIGN CONSULTANTS
Gamma Lighting, Melbourne, VIC Australia
Warren Stegert

SUPPLIERS
Classic Ceramics, Melbourne, VIC Australia
Forbo, Melbourne, VIC Australia
Intergrain, Melbourne, VIC Australia
Bamboo Australia, Melbourne, VIC Australia
Warwick Fiona Jack, Melbourne, VIC Australia
Whitehorse Industries, Melbourne, VIC Australia
George White, Melbourne, VIC Australia
Fusionworks, Melbourne, VIC Australia
Earl Pinto, Melbourne, VIC Australia
Gentech, Melbourne, VIC Australia

Cinq Sens

2450 Laurier Boulevard, Place Ste-Foy, QC, G1V 2L1 Canada

SCOPE OF WORK

Due to the shopping center location the mandate was to design a medico-aesthetic clinic with a retail component catering to a sophisticated Quebec City clientele with high quality expectations. The challenge was to fuse both a clinical and retail environment within a spa ambiance.

GOALS ACHIEVED

Subdividing the space into specific areas created a well-defined customer experience. Three distinct sections have been designed to offer different products and services: a boutique, a manicure/pedicure area and enclosed rooms for health/beauty treatments. The result: Cinq Sens has become a success and has established itself as a trusted beauty destination.

BRAND PROMISE

The goal was to create a holistic experience for the customer regardless of the type of service(s) or product(s) purchased. Cinq Sens' promise was to offer its clients a one-stop beauty destination that sells various skin care products and offers numerous health and beauty treatments.

CUSTOMER JOURNEY

At the storefront sophisticated merchandising of selected cosmetic and skin care products along with modern graphics attract passersby. Inside, experienced estheticians recommend products and introduce the other services. The customer journey is not intended to be a one-time visit, but rather a long-term relationship where clients stay loyal to their esthetician and beauty destination.

BRANDING

The design supports the idea of a clinic meets beauty shop by morphing as a boutique and transitioning into a more spa environment followed by tranquil and sensual rooms. The materials used help support this idea with polished white Carrera marble wall tiles to full height white and black graphics with elusive silhouettes. Sound and scent played an important role in uplifting one's senses. To set the mood, there is upbeat music in the shop, a lounge-y atmosphere in the manicure/pedicure area, and soothing spa melodies in the rooms.

ENVIRONMENTAL GRAPHICS

The backlit visuals atop the display walls strikingly feature brands and catch shopper's attention. A bold and colorful mural in the waiting area successfully separates the reception/cash section from the manicure/pedicure zone while reinforcing the company's brand. The manicure/pedicure zone features an oversized mural of soft daisies and is partially separated from the waiting area with a full-height fuchsia tinted glass panel. Finally, the back section is enclosed with a more clinical setting where each room features a unique sensual silhouette visual.

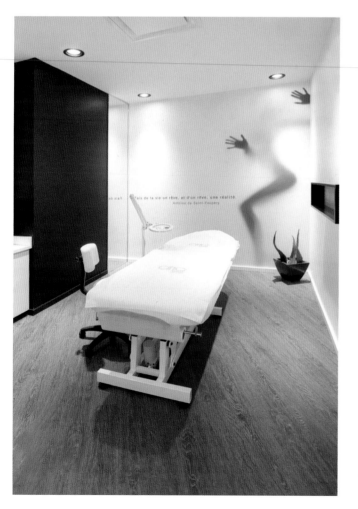

STORE PLANNING

The layout was designed to guide the client from the retail area at the entrance to the esthetics service section then back to the more clinical body and skin treatment area. For privacy, that back section is not visible from the boutique so customers can escape into a tranquil and more discreet clinical environment.

FIXTURING

Custom presentation fixtures were designed to feature various cosmetic and skin care products. All are custom-built and allow for the inserting of a visual merchandise identification tag. Two of the units incorporate a consultation bar where customers can test products. In the spa area, a custom built unit housing four sumptuous chairs heightens the client's experience.

FINISHES

Surface finishes include: chic, high polished white Carrera marble wall tiles; bold, contrasting black and white lacquer finishes; a vibrant, full height tinted fuchsia wall panel; and the understated beauty and warmth of wood pattern porcelain tiled floor

LIGHTING

With a very bright and inviting storefront, decorated with backlit light boxes and a TV screen, the general lighting becomes dimmer as you walk through the space and into the treatment rooms. LED cove lighting is used to highlight the feature graphic wall at the reception while creating a more ambient light in the seating area.

VISUAL MERCHANDISING

All products are merchandised in a refined and uncluttered manner. The boutique is equipped with full-wall length shelves and wide custom-built fixtures to allow an open presentation. White shelving highlights the products and respects the clean and sanitary look of a health and beauty establishment. The treatment rooms are completely void of product with only esthetic equipment visible.

DESIGN FIRM
Ruscio Studio, Montreal, QC Canada

PROJECT DESIGN TEAM
Ruscio Studio, Montreal, QC Canada

ARCHITECT
Max Weber, Architect, Montreal, QC Canada
Max Weber

GENERAL CONTRACTOR
B-Tay Construction Inc., Saint-Nicolas, QC Canada
Michel Drapeau

SUPPLIERS
Tile & Stone:
Italbec, Montreal, QC Canada

Graphics and Lighting:
Lamcom, Montreal, QC Canada

Vinyl Flooring:
Amtico, Calhoun, GA

Plastic Laminate Furniture:
Formica, Saint-Jean-Sur-Richelieu, QC Canada

Wallpaper:
Crown Wallpaper, Montreal, QC Canada

Upholstery:
Designtex, New York, NY

Hermosa Pharmacy

C/Galicia 3. 23100, Mancha Real. Jaén, Spain

GOALS AND OBJECTIVES

The following goals and objectives were successfully achieved: an integrated and complete design of a new brand concept in the Spanish pharmacy sector; has become the reference for pharmacies in and outside Spain despite its location in a small Spanish village; has blended the mood of a local shop with the design of a modern department store; has engaged better employees and improved the product offer attracting the best beauty and healthy brands in the industry.

BRANDING

The concept of Hermosa Pharmacy is " The Healthy Courtyard." The concept was developed on the basis of two characteristic components: a design that derives from the traditional decorated apothecary; and the use of an interior space to sell medicines, lit by natural sunlight that enters through skylights, as well as an area where medicinal plants are grown.

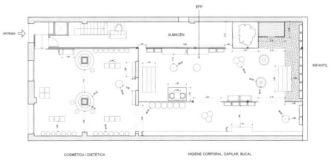

COSMÉTICA / DIETÉTICA   HIGIENE CORPORAL, CAPILAR, BUCAL

ENVIRONMENTAL GRAPHICS

The wayfinding and graphic design were inspired by the "albarellos," the traditional decorated apothecary jars in which, in times gone by, medicinal plants were kept.

STORE PLANNING

The customer journey starts with the façade, a 6x6 meter cross and a show-stopping display of 64 backlit acrylic "albarellos," each one with a different message. The pharmacy is divided into three main areas according to the products/services categories and the desired shopping experience. The entrance feels like a beauty salon. The design of the room for body-care, oral hygiene and dietary products is centered on a wall with niches where the light and the color of the wood are part of the pharmacy's unique identity. Acrylic "albarellos" and "tester" spaces form part of the product presentation, bringing the product closer to the client. Medicine and children's products are sold in a room christened "The Healthy Courtyard."

FINISHES

The materials have been selected to give the impression of a "luxury-eco-chic" pharmacy. Country-style furniture and ambiance mix with glamorous lighting and luxurious surfaces such as Coralwood, Koto Wood and other contemporary materials including concrete, plexi-glass, and artificial grass.

LIGHTING

Light and shadows are key aspects. Natural light harmonizes with electric light. LED lights trace the customer journey by illuminating the ceiling. LEDs are also used inside furniture to highlight the product. The merchandise and walls are illuminated using movable spotlights that provide extra impact thanks to a combination of halogens and halides.

VISUAL MERCHANDISING

Two African Coralwood coated pillars with mirrors, one with a water fountain, offer a fresh and delightful welcome. A collection of circular shelves adorns the walls in the main room. The shadows are part of the image; the product is presented to entice not to overwhelm, to tell a delectable story—your beauty is waiting to be discovered. Medicine and children's products are sold in separate a room. The patio has been converted into a beautiful room with an African Coralwood checkered roof, where the natural light harmonizes with the pharmacy lighting. The cash registers are "albarellos" and the products are presented in "flower beds." There are Provençal style waiting benches, a cabin for pharmaceutical services, and a stall for the promotion of children's products. An external garden for growing medicinal plants, a ball-pit for the younger children to enjoy and an array of photographs of happy children encourage you to browse through the entire Pharmacy.

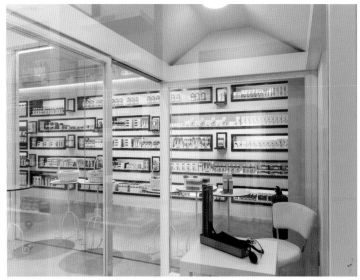

DESIGN FIRM
Marketing-Jazz, Madrid, Spain

PROJECT DESIGN TEAM

Carlos Sanchez de Pedro Aires
Elena de Andres, Concept, Ambient &
Furniture Design, Visual Merchandising
and Overall Creativity Supervision
Natalia Sanchez de Pedro Aires,
Illustration and Sketches
Silvia Teijeiro, Graphic Design
Luis Sanchez de Pedro Aires,
Planimetry and 3D Design
Photography, portraits of employees
and children

ARCHITECT

Technical Architect:

Mr. Pedro Ponce de Leon, Madrid,
Spain

GENERAL CONTRACTOR

Construcciones Romero Vico,
Jaén, Spain
Juan Martin Romero

OUTSIDE DESIGN CONSULTANTS

Product Lighting:

Microlights, Barcelona, Spain
Mrs. Nuria Torrents

Architectural Lighting:

Simon, Madrid, Spain
Mrs. Marta Lozano

SUPPLIERS

Furniture Manufacturer:

Artdemob, Barcelona, Spain

Flooring:

Microfloor, Madrid, Spain

THE BEST PHARMACY STORES IN THE WORLD

Founded by Carlos Aires in 2002, Marketing-Jazz is a leading Spanish visual marketing firm. For the past two years industry professionals have recognized our retail pharmacy projects as being among the world's best.

Our approach to successful pharmacy design is a creative and integrated process utilizing innovative pharmacy design concepts that ultimately increase profits and sales for our clients. We focus on the entire process from store layout and the shopping experience, to branding and communication, to the training of staff in visual merchandising.

Marketing-Jazz closely cooperates with retailers and business leaders/entrepreneurs to create successful venues worldwide.

Please contact Carlos at carlos@marketing-jazz.com or visit our website www.marketing-jazz.com

Creative retail design from Madrid
since 2002

Amouage Flagship Store & Visitor Centre

Oman Perfumery LLC, PO Box 307, CPO 111, Muscat, Oman

SCOPE OF WORK

JHP was commissioned to design a new flagship store and visitor center at their headquarters in Muscat. Owned by the Omani Royal family, the brand is now a truly international business with shops and accounts in 52 countries. The five-year project included the center's architecture, retail design, landscaping, and visitor experience.

GOALS AND OBJECTIVES

The design of the new flagship store and visitor center also included its fragrance manufacturing facility. The objective was to enable the business to increase its production to 20,000 bottles per week from the current 8,000, as well providing a memorable experience for visitors to learn all aspects of perfume creation.

GOALS ACHIEVED

The new retail offer, factory and visitor center is the showpiece the Amouage's growing retail presence. The new retail and factory facility has given Amouage the capacity to produce and sell its products at its current location. It has also helped visitors' understanding of the various stages of perfume manufacturing, from ingredient maceration to bottling and packaging to explaining the perfume extraction process.

BRAND PROMISE

The brand promise of Amouage is a lifestyle sought after by only the most sophisticated and discerning international. The House of Amouage restores artistry to perfumery to create extraordinarily beautiful scents with a distinct point of view and sources the globe for unique and the highest quality of ingredients. The atmosphere therefore created by the design agency is one of an overwhelming sense of luxury, grace and tradition.

CUSTOMER JOURNEY

The space is divided into the flagship store, the factory, and the visitor experience. The retail store contains the full. Visitors arrive in a beautifully appointed orientation room more like the reception area of a luxury hotel than a visitor center, then past the glass walls allowing clear views into the factory to the product gallery area. Customers then move onto the retail space where they are encouraged to handle and test the product and purchase.

BRANDING

The Amouage brand palette was taken into the more industrial aspects of the factory and visitor center. It was expressed liberally in the more luxurious aspects of the visitor center and by way of a slight diversification in the minimalist way it is employed in the retail gallery. Product is displayed in glass boxes in an environment more akin to an art gallery than a retail store. The focus on sourcing only the finest of ingredients in its perfumes is reflected in the choice of very high quality of materials and finishes which the designers used in the scheme.

ENVIRONMENTAL GRAPHICS

The brand has a distinctive logo and this is replicated in various guises, as a screen on the roofline and carved into extremely tall teak entrance doors. The Amouage name means 'wave' hence the signature-curved entrance canopy viewed in the exterior photo. This undulating mirrored roof feature sits alongside the shimmering tiered water feature. A Halo illuminated Amouage shield was also applied to the building in marble.

STORE PLANNING

Beginning at the reception area, the customer journey takes visitors past the factory first, then gallery area, and then onto the retail space. Floor to ceiling windows allow full views into the factory production area. The retail area acts as an elegant gallery for the full product range at the culmination of the journey.

FIXTURING

The museum like space showcases key products in a double height luxury product gallery. The merchandising assembles the various product ranges in an attractive display whilst making it easy to shop, encouraging product testing and interaction with the store staff. The products sit on elegant white tables and counters or are housed in beautiful glass display boxes.

FINISHES

The color palette matches the local stones, sands and color scheme of the desert. The huge circular 'Sinbad' rose window deliberately lets in the blue sky of Oman, whilst the dark timber surround to products and frames reflect the teak of the Omani dows (local boats). Omani Desert Rose marble makes up all external pathways, and is used for the cladding of the new building. Elsewhere, Italian porcelain tile was used throughout along with walnut wood in feature areas such as the boardroom and the CEO's office.

LIGHTING

Lots of natural daylight streams into the building through the use of high-level glazing, glass walls, and roof lights above the retail gallery. Concealed micro LEDs within the slender frame are used to illuminate the product.

VISUAL MERCHANDISING

Visitors can view the factory area creating true retail theatre, thus the essence of the brand is revealed. In the retail area the attention to detail in terms of product display, lighting and careful curating of products is of the very highest standard, appropriate to the expectations from a luxury brand.

SUSTAINABILITY

The designers embraced the building traditions and the architecture of Oman in its development of the factory's exterior and interior design. The walls are as thick maintaining heat in the winter and remaining cool in summer. Natural ventilation is used to let hot air exit and solar paneling was used extensively on the roof.

DESIGN FIRM
JHP, London, UK

PROJECT DESIGN TEAM
Steve Collis, JHP Managing Director
Raj Wilkinson, JHP Managing Director
John McCarthy, Senior Retail Designer
David Crickmore, CEO of Amouage

RETAIL DESIGN TEAM
Raj Wilkinson, JHP Managing Director
John McCarthy, Senior Retail Designer

ARCHITECT
JHP, London, UK

GENERAL CONTRACTOR
Beemco, Muscat
Gilbert Albuquerque

SUPPLIERS
Beemco, Muscat, *managed all supplies of materials, finishes and textures*

Perry Ellis Showroom

1120 Avenue of the Americas, New York, NY

SCOPE OF WORK

In response to growth associated with renewed brand awareness and corporate acquisitions, and motivated by the need to change to a building that better suited their programmatic needs, Perry Ellis International undertook a relocation of its operations from the Grace Building to two floors at the Hippodrome. The space includes new headquarters for Perry Ellis International on the 8th Floor and a brand new 12,000 square foot showroom for the Perry Ellis brand on the 7th Floor.

GOALS AND OBJECTIVES

Perry Ellis sought a flexible and open space to increase collaboration and provide easy access to merchandise with ample space for designer interaction, image boards, pin-up areas and hand-on design activities. The space also needed to accommodate various sized groups for meetings, fashion shows and events.

GOALS ACHIEVED

The successful outcome includes open spaces throughout the showroom to allow a smaller footprint and collaboration between designers and customers. Walls throughout the space adjust and collapse to accommodate various sized groups. The neutral palette allows for a constant update of merchandise and display during the seasonal and brand changes. Workspaces and network connections are available for frequent out of town staff visitors.

BRAND PROMISE

The Perry Ellis brand has always stood for American clothing that synthesizes high style and levity. The new offices and showrooms exhibit the same blend of classicism and style harkening back to the

"Perry Ellis Studio" of the 1980s and is very product focused, as mannequins, staging and product display areas line the conference rooms.

CUSTOMER JOURNEY

Designed as a retail environment, the showroom utilizes a number of features that are currently being developed for stores and shop-in-shops. The aesthetic, graphics and lighting are consistent with that of brick and mortar retail stores, to give customers a similar experience in the showroom environment.

BRANDING

Perry Ellis' brand statement is "Very Perry." The brand's strong showroom design focuses on the classicism presented by the clothing and labels housed under the Perry Ellis International name.

ENVIRONMENTAL GRAPHICS

Directly adjacent to the Perry Ellis International reception area, a half-height, textural wooden maple wall demarcates the entrance to the showroom one floor below—enter the world of Perry. Perry Ellis graphics can be seen throughout the showroom.

STORE PLANNING

The space is designed to accommodate Perry Ellis International on the top floor, while the showroom on the 7th floor is connected through a custom built staircase.

FIXTURING

It was imperative that merchandise hardware and shelving were included in conference rooms as a means for designers to display clothing during meetings.

FINISHES

Throughout the showroom, a number of different materials including metal, glass, wood and stone are utilized to exhibit a distressed, yet polished feel. The finishes are found in doorframes, showroom walls, retail hardware and flooring.

LIGHTING

In a showroom environment, it is important that lighting displays clothing the way it would be showcased in a retail environment. The firm worked closely with lighting consultants to replicate retail lighting in the showroom.

VISUAL MERCHANDISING

Staging areas for mannequins and product display areas are found throughout the showroom to artistically and visually showcase Perry Ellis products.

DESIGN FIRM
TPG Architecture,
New York, NY

PROJECT DESIGN TEAM
Jim Phillips, Principal
Tom Hughes, Studio Head
Ken Tracey, PM
Anthony Simon, Design Director
Kate Kolacki, Designer
Jamie Espiritu, PA

STORE DESIGN TEAM
Niki Varadi

ARCHITECT
TPG Architecture, New York, NY 10010
Jim Phillips

GENERAL CONTRACTOR
Benchmark Builders, Inc.,
New York, NY
Michael J. Trocchia, Senior Project Manager

OUTSIDE DESIGN CONSULTANTS
MEP Engineer:
AMA Consulting Engineers, P.C.,
New York, NY
Maureen Doyle

SUPPLIERS
Furniture Vendor:
The Atlantic Group FPPM, Inc.,
New York, NY
Office Fronts:
Infinium Wall Systems
Movable Partitions:
Modernfold, Inc., Greenfield, IN
Signage:
Coyle & Company Graphics, Inc.,
Holbrook, NY

BUILDING THE FUTURE OF RETAIL DESIGN

The Planning and Visual Education Partnership (PAVE) is the educational foundation for the retail environments industry. It helps to grow a future talent pool and foster professional development in retail design and planning and visual merchandising by:

- awakening students to available industry careers
- providing real-world projects for collegiate curriculum
- encouraging budding talent
- supporting robust collegiate design programs
- recognizing young leaders
- linking job candidates to industry partners

2013 PAVE Student Design Competition Winners:
Top Photo L-R: Quianna Teixeira, Jennifer Bukovec, and Rachel McGarry *Bottom Photo L-R:* Jaemin Song, Lauren Ferrell, and Gabrielle Enzweiler

During the past year, PAVE awarded over $75,000 to students and educational institutions. Programs include two design competitions with worldwide participation, scholarships, design school grants, an internship program, seminars, and a professional recognition program.

Help grow the future of retail design

- Join a PAVE Committee
- Offer an internship
- Fund a single or multi-year scholarship for students
- Make a donation to PAVE
- Purchase a table for the PAVE Gala or sponsor a student to attend
- Sponsor PAVE's Student Design Competition or PAVE the Way 3D Design Challenge

PAVE is a 501(c)(3) educational foundation administered by A·R·E • For more information visit www.paveinfo.org.

4651 Sheridan St., Suite 470, Hollywood, FL 33021 • 954-241-4834 • fax 954-893-8375 • pave@paveinfo.org • www.paveinfo.org

Retail Design Institute

International Student Design
Congratulations to the 2014 First Place Winner

Mandy Green
Interior Design Student
College of Mount St. Joeseph

"Inspired by the farmers market,
Fresh Face is a cosmetics store that focuses on the
environmentally and wellness conscious women".

The Institute is dedicated to educating and attracting the best young talent into the retail design profession

Innovation   Collaboration   Education   Leadership   Credentials

Supporting Student Design Since 1972

Index

FRCH Design Worldwide
311 Elm Street, Suite 600
Cincinnati, OH 45202
513-362-3424
www.frch.com
Liverpool Veracruz El Dorado Pg. 30

-G-

Gensler
2 Harrison Street, Suite 400
San Francisco, CA 94105
415-433-3700
www.gensler.com
Hudson Grace Pg. 76

Gensler
711 Louisiana, Suite 300
Houston, TX 77002
713-356-1397
www.gensler.com
*Charming Charlie - Store of the Future
Pg. 122*

Geyer
Level 6, 259 Collins Street
Melbourne, VIC 3000
Australia
+61 3-9655-9344
www.geyer.com.au
Telstra Retail Store of the Future Pg. 174

GH+A
1100, avenue des Canadiens-de-Montreal
Suite 130
Montreal, QC H3B 2S2
Canada
514-843-5812 x229
info@ghadesign.com
www.ghadesign.com
Pg. 161
Richmond Centre Dining Terrace Pg. 156

Giorgio Borruso Design
333 Washington Boulevard, #352
Marina Del Rey, CA 90292
310-821-9224
elizabeth@borrusodesign.com
borrusodesign.com
Carlo Pazolini Brompton Rd Pg. 100

-H-

Huen
1911 NW Quimby Street
Portland OR 97209
503-224-4836
Info@huenspace.com
www.huenspace.com
Pg. 29
Umpqua Bank San Francisco, Pg. 22

-J-

JHP
Unit 2, 6 Erskine Road
London NW3 3AJ
UK
Austin.m@jhp-design.co.uk
www.jhp-design.co.uk
*Amouage Flagship Store & Visitor Centre
Pg. 208*

-K-

King Retail Solutions
3850 West 1st Avenue
Eugene, OR 97402
541-686-2848
lindsey.muth@kingrs.com
www.kingrs.com
Pg. 131
Fresh St. Market Pg. 126

-L-

LalireMarchArchitects
304 Hudson Street, 6 fl
New York, NY 10013
212-807-1011
lma@laliremarch.com
www.laliremarch.com
Barneys New York Pg. 42

Landini Associates
43 Rainford Street
Surry Hills, Sydney, NSW
Australia
+61 (0)2-9360-3899
studio@landiniassociates.com
www.landiniassociates.com
Pg. 137
No Frills Stratford Pg. 132

Linea Partnership LLP
2110 Tower A Jian Wai SOHO
39 East Third Ring Road, Central
Chaoyang District
Beijing, Chima 100022
86-10-5869-1728
info@lineapartnership.com
www.lineapartnership.com
Lane Crawford Yin Tai Pg. 48

Luxottica Retail Australia Design & Construct
L4/75 Talavera Road
Macquarie Park, NSW 2113
Australia
+61 421-075-197
http://www.luxottica.com.au/
Sunglass Hut Sydney Flagship Pg. 72

-M-

Mark A Steele Photography Inc.
1515D Delashmut Avenue
Columbus, OH 43212
614-291-0519 studio
mark@marksteelephotography.com
www.marksteelephotography.com
Pg. 17

McCall Design Group
550 Kearny Street #950
San Francisco, CA 94108
415-288-8150
www.mccalldesign.com
4information@mccalldesign.com/
Umpqua Bank San Francisco, Pg. 22

MARKETING-JAZZ.
C/ Huelva 16, Estudio 54
Madrid, 28100
Spain
34-6-255-69697
carlos@marketing-jazz.com
www.marketing-jazz.com
Pg. 207
Hermosa Pharmacy Pg. 202

Mondo Manniquins
300 Karin Lane
Hicksville NY 11801
516-935-7700
(Showroom)
121 West 27th St., 2nd floor
New York, NY 10001
sales@mondomannequins.com
www.mondomannequins.com
Pg. 8

MNA
127 W 24th Street, Floor 7
New York, NY 10011
212-675-2285
info@mnarch.com
www.mnarch.com
Patagonia Meatpacking Pg. 88
Tommy Bahama Bar, Restaurant and Store
Pg. 94
Patagonia Bowery Pg. 110

-P-

P+F ARCHITETTI
Aldo Parisotto+ Massimo Formenton
via Marcona 3
20129 Milano
Italy
+39-02-54050276
Via N. Sauro 15
35139 Padova
Italy
+39-049-8755255
www.studioparisottoeformenton.it
info@studioparisottoeformenton.it
Nespresso Boutique Bar Toronto Pg. 164

Pinto Tuncer Pty Ltd.
14-16 Sackville Street
Collingwood, VIC 3066
Australia
+61 3-9416-2023
ilker@pintotuncer.com
www.pintotuncer.com
Qi Master Reflexology Pg. 192

-R-

RCS Innovations
7075 West Parkland Court
Milwaukee, WI 53223
414-354-6900
larry.laguardia@RCSinnovations.com
www.RCSinnovations.com
Pg. 184
AT&T Store of the Future Pg. 179

rkd retail/iQ
GPF Witthayu Towers
Suite 703-704 Tower A
93/1 Wireless Road
Lumpini, Pathumwan
Bangkok, 10330
Thailand
+662-255-3155
talk2us@rkdretailiq.com
www.rkdretailiq.com
Pg. 59
DFS Galleria, Scottswalk Pg. 54
DFS Wine & Cigars Pg. 138

Ruscio Studio
2197 Sherbrooke Street East
Montreal, QC H2K 1C8
Canada
514-276-0600
marketing@rusciostudio.com
www.rusciostudio.com
Cinq Sens Pg. 198

Richter+Ratner
45 West 36th Street, 12th floor
New York, NY 10018
212-936-4500
www.richterratner.com
info@richterratner.com
Pg. 10

-S-

Sanzpont [arquitectura]
Fluviá 139, 2-3
Barcelona 8020
Spain
+52 998-8845238
Av. Tulum Núm.
192, Mza 17,
Supermanzana 4,
Cancún, C.P77500
México
arquitectura@sanzpont.com
www.sanzpont.com
Real Madrid Official Store Gran Vía 31
Pg. 104

SHE-Architekten
Hamburg, Germany
http://www.she-architekten.com/
t.boutique & t.bar Pg. 170

Shea, Inc.
10 South 8th Street
Minneapolis, MN 55402
612-339-2257
info@sheadesign.com
www.sheadesign.com
Marin Restaurant & Bar Pg. 150

Stylmark Inc
PO Box 32006
6536 Main Street NE
Minneapolis, MN 55432
763-574-1415
info@stylmark.com
www.stylmark.com
Pg. 21

-T-

T-square Design Consultants
1130 North Avenue
New Rochelle, NY 10804
914-637-8024
tsquaredesignusa@gmail.com
http://www.tsquare-usa.com/
CHANEL at Macy's Herald Square Pg. 60

t.lovers GmbH
Erikastr. 53
Hamburg, 20251
Germany
49-17-124-4524 e+011
http://www.t-lovers.de
t.boutique & t.bar Pg. 170

TID International
TID Associates
22B Mosque Street
Singapore 059502
+65-6225-7747
www.tidassociates.com
audrey@tidassociates.com
DFS Galleria, Scottswalk Pg. 54

TNB Design
6 Broadhurst Place
Baulkham Hills, NSW 2153
Australia
timbennett@optusnet.com.au
Sunglass Hut Sydney Flagship Pg. 72

Toshiba Global Commerce Solutions
3039 Cornwallis Road, Bldg 307
Research Triangle Park, NC 27709
800-426-4968
www.toshibagcs.com
Pg. 20

TPG Architecture
31 Penn Plaza
132 W 31st Street
New York, NY 10001
212-768-0800
www.tpgarchitecture.com
Perry Ellis Showroom Pg. 214

Tran Dieu & Associates Inc
50 Weybright Court, Unit 4
Scarborough, ON M1S 5A8
Canada
416-298-6370
JaBistro Pg. 146

TRIADmanufacturing
4321 Semple Avenue
St Louis, MO 63120
314.381.5280 ext 1112
www.triadmfg.com
info@triadmfg.com
Pg. 6

Trust Iluminacao
R. da Consolacao 2180/86
Sao Paulo, Brazil
55 11-3231-1100
marketing@trustiluminacao.com.br
www.trustiluminacao.com.br
Pg. 12

Turner Fleischer Architects Inc.
67 Lesmill Road
Toronto, ON M3B 2T8
Canada
416-425-2222
toronto@turnerfleischer.com
www.turnerfleischer.com
No Frills Stratford Pg. 132

-U-
Urban Design Group Architects Ltd.
1140 W Pender Street,
Vancouver, BC V6E 4G1
Canada
604-687-2334
urbandesign@udga.com
www.udga.com
Kung Pao Wok Pg. 163

-Y-
Yabu Pushelberg
88 Prince Street, 2nd floor
New York, NY 10012
212-226-0808
infoNYC@yabupushelberg.com
www.yabupushelberg.com
Barneys New York Pg. 42

Yabu Pushelberg
55 Booth Avenue
Toronto, ON M4M 2M3
Canada
416-778-9779
infoTO@yabupushelberg.com
www.yabupushelberg.com
Lane Crawford Yin Tai Pg. 48